The Team: Explorations in Group Process

Chuck Kormanski
Penn State University, Altoona

LOVE PUBLISHING COMPANY®
Denver • London • Sydney

To my wife, Lue,
A true partner in
love and work

Published by Love Publishing Company
Denver, Colorado 80237

Copyright © 1999 Love Publishing Company
Printed in the U.S.A.
ISBN 0-89108-260-3
Library of Congress Catalog Card Number 98–65332

Contents

FIGURES

TABLES

Preface

My professional career for the past 35 years has involved teaching, counseling, and consulting. My major research interest has been group, team, and organizational development. This book draws on my experiences in those areas. Having an early influence in promoting my interest in group, team, and organizational development was my participation in workshops conducted by the National Training Labs (NTL) and University Associates (now Pfeiffer & Co.). Training experiences with Herb Otto, Bill Pfeiffer, Paul Hersey, Ken Blanchard, and Marvin Weisbord were particularly meaningful.

The heart of this book is an integration of a series of models and theories to provide an understanding of the dynamics of change and how a team approach can be used to influence the change process. The group development models of Tuckman, Bion, and Schutz have been around since I began my research. Theories of organizational development with roots in the early work of Lewin, Barnard, and Likert are still evolving. More recent contributions, typically using systems theory as a basis, include those of Barker, Wheatley, Senge, and Weisbord. Attention to the individual has occurred with insight into motivation (Maslow), power (French and Raven), and personality (Jung).

The models that were critical for me in understanding team dynamics were Tuckman's stages of group development and the continuing work on leadership by Hersey and Blanchard. The team development rating scale that my colleague Andy Mozenter and I created was built on Tuckman's group development model and Hersey/Blanchard's situational leadership model.

Prominent in this book are four fictional characters who are composites of my colleagues, students, and friends. They provide a common thread throughout the book and add a personal dimension for the reader. The team experiences described are also composites except for the case studies in Chapter 8. For those case study data and experiences, I am indebted to Dr. Wayne Henderson and the Chestnut Ridge School District Strategic Planning Team, John Schraff and the Altoona-Blair County Chamber of Commerce Leadership Blair County Program, Dr. LeeAnn Eschbach and the Executive Boards of the Pennsylvania Counseling Association, and Dr. Bill Englebret and the Penn

State Altoona Third Shift Maintenance Continuous Quality Improvement Team.

Who should read this book? Although I wrote this book for counselors and psychologists working in schools and private practice settings who deliver counseling and therapy services, it is applicable for any professional who desires an understanding of task accomplishment through teamwork. Graduate students, in particular, will benefit from its comprehensive introduction to group process. The integrative model presented in the book provides a historical context for group, team, and organizational development and has applications for issues of diversity and personality.

Of course, the book is also relevant to leaders of all types, including parents, teachers, community volunteers, coaches, clergy, and politicians. I strove to demonstrate that all of us can become effective leaders and effective team members. Further, all of us can continue to develop and mentor individuals to replace us as leaders as we go about our work with a contagious passion.

The book begins with the introduction of four individuals who, in the process of strengthening their interpersonal relationships, focus on a task and form a team to achieve it. Chapter 1 explores groups and teams, their goals, how teams fit into our society's changing value priorities, and the use of theory for understanding reality. Chapter 2 examines four models of group development, each supported by a personal application experience described by one of the fictional characters. Chapter 3 provides an analysis of change and conflict and how they are managed in groups. To make the discussion more concrete, the fictional characters show how the application experiences they described in Chapter 2 have continued to evolve in dynamic ways that require leadership interventions.

Chapter 4 presents a model of leadership and includes a discussion of knowledge, skills, motivation, and power. Chapter 5 extends the previous presentation to leadership style by examining team member readiness and team leader task and relationship behaviors. Specific attention is given to matching leadership style with readiness levels, motivational needs, group development stages, and power bases. As before, the fictional characters describe personal applications and relevant experiences.

Chapter Six applies models and theories presented earlier in the book to the process of team building. A team development rating scale is introduced and used to assess team effectiveness. A variety of teams are examined utilizing their team development rating scores over time and the resulting change patterns. Chapter 7 focuses on team member diversity issues. Developmental models of social identity, racial-ethnic identity, gender identity, and sexual identity are reviewed and related to group development stages. Personality types and temperaments are explored from both leader and team member perspectives using the theories of Carl Jung, Isabel Briggs Myers, and David Keirsey.

Chapter 8 describes team performance through the presentation of four case studies, one involving the executive board of a state professional counseling association, one involving the strategic planning team of a school district, another involving participants in a community leadership program conducted by a local chamber of commerce, and the last involving a continuous quality improvement team at a university. Chapter 9 concludes the book by encouraging the reader to use teamwork to build a process model, scan the environment for trends, engage in action planning, and live a vision.

Acknowledgments

My own professional development and many of the concepts in this book are the result of a continuous dialogue with friends and colleagues. My work has been enriched by the time I have spent "hanging out" with Richard Hayes, Sam Gladding, Bree Hayes, Bob Conyne, Michael Hutchins, Ann Vernon, Don C. Lock, Diana Hulse-Killacky, Quincy Moore, Rex Stockton, Jesse DeEsch, Holly Forrester-Miller, Becky Schumacher, and Andy Horne, and I am indebted to all of them.

I also want to thank my staff assistants Linda Kitt, Kim Stever, Linda Nedimyer, and Karen Clites, who contributed over time to the preparation of the manuscript, and to Thomas Love and the editorial team at Love Publishing. Finally, I am grateful for the support of my family and the collaborative contributions made by my wife, Lue.

Introduction

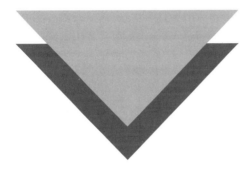

I invent nothing. I rediscover.
—Auguste Rodin

*D*uring the lull following a busy day of conference programs and before an evening of networking and social activities, four friends from the same geographic area sat together in a hotel lobby sharing some of the highlights of the first few days of this annual event. All were professional counselors and had been friends and colleagues for a number of years, but each had found a niche in a different work setting. As a result, their get-togethers and discussions while attending meetings were always lively and engaging, involving a wide diversity of ideas and perspectives.

▼ THE GROUP

Grace, a guidance counselor in a rural public school district, frequently organized the get-togethers. She was dependable and consistently able to provide a structure that made others feel comfortable and welcome. One could count on Grace to take care of the details of any event and be an empathetic hostess. She was active in a number of community service organizations and had developed an award-winning career guidance program in her school.

Alex had been the director of a career development center at a small college but, with time, had found the position too dull and routine. Five years ago, he became the human resources manager in a moderate-size retail corporation. His interest in careers and group work along with his counseling background proved to be an ideal match with the organization, whose major human resources concerns were improving communication and reducing the conflicts associated with rapid change. He was the free spirit of the foursome.

Irma and two colleagues operated a community counseling service. Irma specialized in family and marriage counseling, focusing much of her high energy on understanding people. Others saw her as imaginative and inspirational. She was adept at both individual and group therapy. Irma provided the quartet with an enthusiasm for living and a deep appreciation for the individual person.

Ron was currently serving as the chair of the counselor education department at the only university in the area. Viewed as an innovator and critical thinker, he brought a serious determination to the group.

His understanding of theory and conceptual models proved useful for integrating discussion ideas and developing broad perspectives. Ron viewed learning as the means of obtaining the most critical set of skills needed to live a fulfilling life and viewed group dynamics as the process for maintaining the energy needed for this complex task.

On this particular day, when the group met to talk about the conference programs, Grace initiated the discussion by commenting that, for her, the most interesting applications offered by the conference presenters involved the use of groups and group process. She noted that many of the major challenges she currently faced in her job required interacting with more people, having limited resources, and being under specific time constraints. In addition, accountability demands were increasing.

Ron pointed out that 20 years ago group process in the counseling profession received attention only in counseling groups, therapy groups, and growth or encounter groups, and in business and industry it received attention only in training and development units. He suggested that counseling groups recognized both the task and the relationship dimension of group process but gave more emphasis to relationship behaviors; business and industrial groups reversed this emphasis.

Irma noted that as business and industry became more aware of the importance of relationships in organizational and leadership development, the counseling profession was learning about long-range planning and management by objectives. As a result, there had been an increased balance between attention to task and attention to relationship functions in both arenas.

Alex suggested that the increased use of strategic planning in all organizations had renewed the focus upon task-oriented groups and the need to involve individuals at all levels of the organization in those groups. He mentioned that the total quality management emphasis on service and continuous quality improvement had not only maintained the focus upon tasks but had brought attention to the use of teams to handle complex problems over an extended time frame. He concluded that this extensive use of teamwork had necessitated a concern for both the task and the relationship demands of groups.

Grace stated that another contemporary trend was the increased interest by organizations in managing change and increasing learning opportunities. Ron added that the slow, gradual change that took place in organizations in past decades had accelerated to a rapid pace that rarely allowed for organizational relaxation. He commented that in an effort to gain increased control over change, organizations on the cutting edge were building learning systems and involving everyone in the change process.

Irma quickly pointed out that if everyone were to be a part of the process, the increasing diversity of the workforce would present some major challenges involving inclusion and involvement issues. Alex added that positive team interaction would depend on an understanding of a variety of identity issues including those related to social, racial-ethnic, gender, and sexual orientation. All of these identity issues involved strong emotional content and numerous stereotypes.

All agreed that the trends they had been seeing suggested a number of new roles and possible careers that had, as a central core, group and team development processes. "Group counselor, group facilitator, team leader, and group work specialist are commonly recognized roles in counseling services," Irma said, "but the recent attention to group process as a key dynamic of change and the increased need for leadership abilities to influence the change process have caused renewed interest in the group process functions of observation, facilitation and consultation."

"As a result," Ron said, "a variety of different settings in both education and business are increasing the use of process observers, process facilitators, and process consultants." He added that these roles often appeared as new positions, but in reality they were composed of the same core of knowledge and skills that contributed to the emergence and subsequent development of group dynamics.

There appeared to be some consensus among the foursome that groups and teams were being formed everywhere. Although the topic was intriguing and the discussion lively, time soon ran out. Ron suggested that the group might want to do some informal research on groups and group processes and meet in a few weeks to share their findings. Grace and Irma volunteered to coordinate the selection of topics to avoid duplication, and Alex agreed to copy and distribute the find-ings of each member prior to their next get-together.

For the next meeting, each would prepare a brief summary of their research efforts. Grace would write about the difference between groups and teams. Alex chose to investigate team goals. Irma planned to examine the changing nature of U.S. culture and values. Ron decided to research the use of theories and models to increase understanding and improve performance. Their summaries follow.

▼ GROUPS VERSUS TEAMS

Group development is a naturally occurring process that involves three or more individuals interacting together for a period of time. How the group develops and how long it takes for the group to meet its goals are directly related to the interaction and involvement of the leader and the group members. This process is called group dynamics. When the process involves specific tasks, the term *group work* is frequently used. Group work, then, is a process for bringing individuals together to work on shared tasks and to develop supportive relationships.

All teams are groups; however, the reverse may not be true. Some groups technically cannot be called teams. Reilly and Jones (1974) described four essential criteria that must be present for a group to be called a team. The team members must have shared goals, be commit-ted to work toward those goals, be willing to work interdependently, and be accountable to the organization. A basketball team is an excel-lent example. The team has a reason to work together, which is speci-fied by team goals and an overall purpose. A lack of commitment to the team efforts creates tension and reduces overall effectiveness. Team members have specific assignments for which each is independently responsible, but each individual must also depend upon other team members to complete his or her assignments. Hence, interdependency exists. Finally, basketball teams usually operate within the framework of an organization, such as a league, a school, or a sponsor.

Teams are thus differentiated from groups in that they possess the four essential elements of goals, commitment, interdependence, and accountability. Examples of groups that are not teams include the following: a group of workers who meet daily for their coffee break but who have no defined goals and no accountability for what happens during their meeting; a monthly coin club composed of individual collectors who are not accountable to a higher organization; a group of pageant contestants who are working independently to win and who have little commitment to the group if it lessens their chances of winning; and office staff members who do not volunteer for, but are assigned to, a training program (Kormanski & Mozenter, 1987).

▼ TEAM GOALS

Teams, like groups, are expected to accomplish assigned and chosen tasks and to provide for all members an environment that is supportive and nurturing. New integrative structures suggested in the literature encourage the combining of what were previously considered opposites, such as a focus on group task and a focus on group relationship. Indeed, a blend of opposites has always been a characteristic of teams, which seek to achieve a state of interdependence, being highly dependent and highly independent simultaneously. Team members are typically not only responsible for making specific contributions but must also rely on fellow team members to contribute as well in order to accomplish team objectives. Maslow (1971) has called this phenomenon *transcending dichotomies.*

Another dichotomy challenging teams is the requirement to think both operationally and strategically. Operational thinking addresses the needs of the present. It involves issues that are confronting individuals now, that have narrow impact, that require small changes, and for which there is an obvious solution. Strategic thinking focuses on the future. It involves issues that will confront individuals a few years from now, that have a broad impact, that require major changes, and for which the solution is unclear (Bryson, 1988).

Paralleling the operational and strategic thinking dichotomy is the dual role of team leadership. Effective team leaders provide both transactional leadership and transformational leadership. Whereas transactional leadership manages the current situation, transformational leadership influences the future. Through the former, the team leader guides members in completing tasks using their current skills; through the latter, the leader influences and inspires members to grow and seek out new and exciting challenges (Burns, 1978).

▼ CHANGING VALUE PRIORITIES

As the cultural values of U.S. society changed from the "selfish seventies" to the "concerned eighties," greater emphasis was placed on personal fulfillment, and an increased concern for others became more prominent (Schnall, 1981). This allocentricism has evolved into an acceptance among most individuals of personal responsibility for the world and its inhabitants.

In the 1990s, the criteria for success continue to change. More attention is now being paid to job-related creativity, interdependence, and freedom as well as to such intangible factors as health, education, family, and leisure time. In general, individuals are not afraid of hard work, but they also seek increased appreciation for their efforts and more involvement in the decision-making process. The growth of the total quality management movement provides an example of values translated into action in the workplace. Employees meet on a regular basis to analyze a work-related problem and suggest solutions. W. Edwards Deming, the founder of the quality improvement movement, viewed the team as the center of the continuous quality improvement process (Walton, 1990). As a result, most organizations are now providing training in teamwork and group dynamics to all employees.

Senge (1990) identified five disciplines critical to creating a learning organization. The fifth discipline is systems thinking, the integrative glue that binds the other four disciplines into a power focus on learning and influencing change. The initial four disciplines are personal mastery, mental models, shared vision, and team learning.

Personal mastery involves acquiring knowledge, developing skills, tapping into motivation, and applying those components to solve problems. Mental models determine how we make sense out of the world and are created over time by our culture and personal experiences. A shared vision provides focus, energy, and a direction for organizations and groups. Team learning offers opportunities for all members to contribute and support through dialogue and discussion.

Systems thinking is characterized by interdependent working relationships, clear structural models, open systems, multiple solutions for problems, and a balanced plan for change that considers both structures and people (Fuqua & Kurpius, 1993). The systems theory approach creates a link between task and process (Senge, 1990). Unlike an analytic approach, which attempts to understand the whole by studying each individual part, this theory views the system as a whole, stressing the understanding of task complexity and process relationships.

Solomon (1977) identified five values held by most people in our society that represent implicit assumptions about human nature and organizational life. These values underlie the strategies used in team-building efforts. They include a belief in and an advocacy of democratic society, freedom of choice, scientific inquiry, a healthy organization, and interpersonal knowledge. Peters and Waterman (1982) cited the values of quality, innovativeness, informality, customer service, and concern for people. As a team operates within an organization, the role of leadership is to instill and protect the values of the organization (Burns, 1978; Selznick, 1957); the role of the team is to act on those values.

▼ USE OF THEORY

In its purest sense, theory is speculation and contemplation. Facts are analyzed and organized based on their relationship to one another, and general or abstract principles are developed that suggest explanations and offer understanding in order to reduce confusion and uncertainty. Theories also provide insight and direction when one is confronted with action choices, as well as increase one's confidence in the selected choice. The more theories to which one has access, the more alternatives one has from which to choose (Bolman & Deal, 1984). An examination of available theories of group development is a prerequisite to understanding group process and team development.

Unfortunately, theories may meet all of the aforementioned criteria and not be accurate. Consider the following example. When the early cave people first encountered lightning, uncertainty and fear were the dominant emotions. A spiritual leader provided a theory and an explanation. The "sky gods" were angry because there had not been enough sacrifices. Sacrifices were quickly made to appease the gods. The use of the theory resulted in three important outcomes. People redirected their energy into meaningful action; anxiety levels were decreased; and individuals began to feel more secure. The cave people perceived themselves as more competent, more confident, and more comfortable. The storm passed, and when the sun returned, all felt rewarded and celebrated. Eventually, a new theory came along that made more sense and led to the belief in a new explanation. At that point, what is now commonly called a paradigm (i.e., theory or model) shift occurred (Barker, 1992).

Peter Vaill (1989) used the term *practice theory* for something that looks like a formal theory but is not. He described a practice theory as being based on experience, not systematic research. In essence, it is a mental map of important concepts that may suggest possible research efforts. Weisbord (1987), examining productive workplaces, used some practice theories of Kurt Lewin to demonstrate what actually makes a workplace productive. When followed by research, practice theories have the potential to produce formal theories.

One can find practice theories, like diamonds in the rough, scattered throughout the literature as well as mentioned at conferences, workshops, and seminars. With a little polish, these gems often illuminate that which had been unnoticed or hidden or is soon to appear. The key is to recognize insight so that learning can occur in simple observations and relationships. A practice theory may have to be adapted to a specific situation. But each new application may suggest additional shaping and contribute to the overall growth and development of a formal theory.

▼ THE GROUP BECOMES A TEAM

The group of Grace, Alex, Irma, and Ron met and discussed their findings. At the meeting, Ron mentioned that the brief attempt at writing was helpful to him in clarifying his thoughts and suggested that they might combine their research and writing efforts to produce something more substantial and informative over time. All but Ron had, at one time or another, complained about not having opportunities to write and do research. Although writing was a critical component of Ron's position at the university, he was eager to take on another writing task, envisioning an insightful manuscript from a variety of work setting perspectives being created by the group. Irma contributed the fact that all had meaningful experiences to share. Alex liked the idea of a new challenge. Grace saw the project as a method for teaching others about what they were learning. All were soon convinced that they should pursue the project.

The group now had a shared goal. All were motivated and committed to working toward that goal. Goal achievement appeared possible through an interdependent work effort. The only ingredient lacking for the group to become a team was accountability. Alex suggested a simple form of performance contracting, a strategy used in his company to improve supervisor-employee work relationships and productivity. A contract would be written specifying the tasks, objectives, and time lines for each team member, including shared leadership roles that could be rotated among the four. All would put their integrity on the line with their signatures. Ron noted that he had used a similar technique with graduate students who were writing dissertations. Grace had used a contracting process to help teachers at her school work with misbehaving students, and Irma had her clients in therapy construct personal contracts to change undesired behaviors. During subsequent meetings, the contract was written and signed, and the group officially became a team. A brainstorming session provided a number of interesting names for the team, but no name excited everyone. During the session, group decision making appeared more difficult than any of the members had expected. As the meeting time elapsed, Alex decided to use "The Team" as a heading for the contract.

A month later, the team, as the group now called itself, met to continue forward with their research and writing effort. Each member had agreed to bring for discussion a short description of a group that had become a team. All thought this exercise would be a logical step for understanding the group process in team development.

Grace presented her description first, since hers was of a team just beginning a task. "I am working with an old team on a new and very different project. We have recently completed an assessment of our community resources. We are now going to begin a parent involvement task force. The task is challenging, and creative problem solving will be critical. In past efforts of the team, there were few choices and there was very little flexibility. Our current project will require some talents that the team members have not used recently. In particular, everyone will need to be assertive and visionary. I am concerned about increasing the motivational level of the team in addition to getting the project completed in a superior fashion."

Alex was eager to talk next. "I am facilitating a continuous quality improvement team at work. Our current project is to redesign our employee lounge. The team members disagree about the importance of the project and, therefore, the time needed to complete it. One group of team members sees the task as helpful but not essential to the organization. They want to finish the project adequately but quickly. A second set of team members wants to complete the task comprehensively with the high-quality characteristic of past team performance. A third group is trying to develop a compromise. A few members have not expressed opinions and are attempting to stay out of the debate. I would like to resolve the matter and get the team to reach a consensus or at least a compromise. My personal preference is for a quality effort."

After hearing about the conflict in Alex's team, Irma shared her experience. "I am chairing a committee that is planning a state counseling conference. The team has recently resolved a volatile disagreement regarding the appropriate strategy to use in the implementation of a major goal. The members decided to reduce costs by using local presenters instead of those from outside the area who require more expensive arrangements. With that conflict behind us, I want to move forward as quickly as possible. However, the group appears somewhat hesitant and continues to look to me for direction. Members appear to be capable of continuing the task but are concerned about how much time will be required of them. Some have begun the work independently and in pairs. Although I see some progress, I would like a more unified effort."

Finally, Ron provided a description of a team that had almost completed its work. "I am leading a team developing a strategic planning update at my university. The team appears to be cohesive and unified regarding the current project of creating a new vision. All members are competent to complete the task. The implementation and evaluation phase will be critical and will impact the total organization. Our current goals are challenging but realistic. So far, quality standards have been maintained. I am now eager to complete the project at this high level of performance."

As the group discussed their varied experiences, Ron noted that each of the teams they had described appeared to be at a different stage in its development. Grace pointed out that they were dealing with different tasks as well. Irma added that the relationships among the members of each team elicited different emotions. Ron suggested that different actions were probably needed to ensure the healthy development of each team.

Irma asked everyone to think about what other factors they should examine to increase their understanding of how groups become effective teams. Alex contributed the idea that conflict frequently occurs and challenges teams during periods of rapid change. Grace added that leadership was critical and involved knowledge acquisition, skill development, and an understanding of both motivation and power. Ron mentioned that leaders often had different styles and that some leaders were able to change styles as the situations in which they were involved changed.

Alex redirected the discussion from focusing on leadership to focusing on membership. He noted that sometimes individuals were effective leaders but that very few people knew how to be good team members. He also noted that the learning styles of the team members had to be taken into account. He, for example, learned best by doing; he needed physical involvement and activity. He admitted to having a short attention span, being restless in highly structured learning situations, and thriving on the verbal and visual. He perceived himself as immediate and resourceful but often not a good team member—"although I am working on that last aspect," he noted.

Irma entered the discussion by pointing out that she needed interaction with other people to learn. She had a preference for group discussion, reflection, and one-to-one dialogue. She expressed a need for acceptance and support from others and worked better in cooperative rather than competitive situations. She admitted to giving more attention to people than tasks. "I like the interaction of the team," she concluded.

Ron suggested a third learning style by describing his need for abstract ideas. He had a preference for theories, models, speculations, and possibilities. For him, principles, logic, and modern technology were appealing. "I do overlook the practical and specific," he admitted. "I like to set high standards, focus on achievement, and design systems."

Grace suggested a fourth learning style, which emphasized a structured learning situation that encouraged responsibility, dependability, and organization. She preferred directive instruction and scheduled, concrete activities. She admitted to sometimes being too rigid and being reluctant to make rapid, complex changes. "I appreciate having well-defined directives and standards," she noted.

Irma concluded the discussion by suggesting that all of the ideas raised could provide insight about how to build effective and productive teams. The team's research topic began to take shape, and each team member left the meeting eager to continue their research and already anticipating their next get-together.

Group Development Stages

2

There is nothing so practical as a good theory.

—Kurt Lewin

*T*he team decided that they would meet for two 3-hour sessions each month. For their first few get-togethers Ron selected the place to meet; Grace organized an informal agenda; Alex agreed to produce a written summary; and Irma volunteered to coordinate the refreshments. As the team gathered for their first bimonthly meeting, they planned to tackle the topic of group development.

Grace noted that their discussion of teams at the previous gathering had been both helpful and stimulating. As the team she was coordinating at work was just beginning its task, she found it insightful to listen to the descriptions of the other teams, which were further along, and their dynamics. "Talking about teams in various stages of development last time allowed me to formulate some ideas about what might happen to my team as we continue to interact," she remarked.

Ron commented that the descriptions of the other group members' teams mirrored the dynamics he had observed in his group, which had been together for some time. He added the insight that even though there were broad, thematic dynamics, they did appear to be sequential in nature. "The specific dynamics are probably unique for each team," he noted. He suggested that identifying the themes and their sequence would be a logical next step.

Irma spoke next. She commented that in addition to being thematic and sequential, this process appeared to be developmental. "If Ron's observations are accurate," she noted, "we as a group will need to wrestle with each of the sequential, thematic issues and manage each one before proceeding to the next in the developmental process." She added, "My team worked at getting organized, like Grace's team is doing now. Then we struggled with some major conflict issues similar to those Alex's team is experiencing. I hope my team will soon become as productive as Ron's team." In summarizing, Irma commented that she felt the conflict her team had experienced and the members' current indecisiveness in moving forward were essential ingredients of team development.

For Alex, the discussion during the previous get-together offered some hope as well as an action oriented direction. He realized that the group conflict his team was experiencing was normal and could be managed in ways that would promote growth and development. "It appears that there are some broad stages that describe how teams change over time and that these stages are characterized by being thematic, sequential, and developmental," he concluded. He suggested that exploring some theories about group development could provide insight about what to expect and how to prepare for the dynamics that normally occur as a team moves from getting organized to achieving successful outcomes.

Each member of the team agreed to research a particular theory of group development. Ron selected the classic work of Bruce Tuckman (1965). Alex selected the work of W. R. Bion (1961), which was influenced by psychodynamic theory. Irma's interest in people led her to Bill Schutz (1958) and his fundamental interpersonal relations orientation theory. Grace chose to research the work of Roy Lacoursiere (1980) which is often used as a model for team building. They compiled the following results.

▼ TUCKMAN'S DEVELOPMENTAL SEQUENCE

Bruce Tuckman (1965) suggested a four-stage model of group development based upon his extensive review of 50 studies. He added a fifth stage following his examination of an additional 22 studies (Tuckman & Jensen, 1977). He named the five stages forming, storming, norming, performing, and adjourning. Each stage had both a task component and a relationship component, which paralleled the early development of leadership theory.

The forming stage involves the group getting organized. It is a movement toward awareness of roles, rules, and standards. From a task perspective, there is an orientation to the group goals and a testing of boundaries. The relationship perspective is characterized by a dependency upon leadership and influential group members. Getting oriented to the task and getting acquainted with others in the group are the first steps in the group development process.

As orientation and dependency issues are resolved, a storming stage begins to emerge. This movement toward conflict is a natural phenomenon that initially appears as resistance to the task and hostility among group members. However, it also brings to light different viewpoints, diversity, and additional choices. It is not always loud and obvious, it may surface quietly as stubbornness and avoidance. The challenge for the group is to manage the conflict and emotions. The counterdependence of this stage frequently results in a rebellion against the leadership. Working through this stage requires an active commitment to the group process and a desire to seek common ground among the group members.

Effective conflict management and the clarification of task and roles pave the way for the norming stage. Behaviors change from competitive to collaborative and the atmosphere becomes one of cooperation. Independent opinions are expressed more freely, and communication channels open to facilitate task accomplishment. Group cohesion serves as the relationship glue that binds the group more closely together. The sharing of information promotes synergy. The increase in harmony and openness supports a more positive morale, which fosters team-building efforts. Group unity and shared responsibility lead to decision making by consensus and promote more democratic leadership styles.

The performing stage is characterized by functional role relatedness. Thus, the group can support instead of hinder task work through the use of function-oriented roles. The theme is a productivity work effort.

The adjourning stage brings a group or a task to closure. The process involves termination of the task and disengagement from relationships. Typically, groups plan some type of recognition for participation and achievement. In addition, group members need opportunities to say good-bye. Often rituals and ceremonies are used to provide a set time frame and a specific ending point.

▼ APPLYING TUCKMAN'S MODEL

Ron described a 10-week, one-credit seminar entitled Interpersonal Relations that was offered to students at his university. Over 100 students participated in this small-group experience during a 2-year period. Each seminar participant kept a log. Logs were to include personal thoughts, viewpoints, and feelings about the content and the process of the seminar. Participants were encouraged to evaluate and comment upon their own participation in the seminar experiences and their interaction with others. Each session of the seminar included a brief lecture (15 to 30 minutes) on a relevant topic, such as personal awareness, self-concept, communication skills, values, and conflict, and one or two experiential learning activities (45 to 60 minutes). Participants contracted to change an interpersonal behavior and to measure their progress toward that goal during the seminar.

Participant logs were examined for evidence of the thematic content of the stages of group development. The Tuckman model terminology was used to label the themes. Specific attention was given to locating forming examples during weeks 1 and 2; storming examples during weeks 3, 4, and 5; norming examples during weeks 5, 6, and 7; performing examples during weeks 8 and 9; and adjourning examples during week 10.

Early sessions of the seminar included activities that examined the wants and expectations of group members. The group leaders provided opportunities for the members to talk informally with one another and informed them of the basic format and structure of future seminar meetings. In addition, skills in feedback and self-disclosure were taught. Student log comments reflected the thematic content of the forming stage. As can be seen in the following comments, uncertainty about the tasks and hesitancy about relationships were major concerns.

STAGE 1: FORMING
Orientation and Dependency Examples

▼ "I am hoping the class will help me to adjust my behavior patterns, so I'll get along better with others."
▼ "That's what the class is all about—talking to each other and learning to relate better and easier."
▼ "I am hoping this course will improve me as a person."
▼ "I got to meet new people who are in some of my classes who never spoke to me, and now they talk to me."
▼ "This is my first experience with this kind of class."
▼ "I'm a little worried about what I've gotten myself into."

▼ "I may have trouble in this class, since I don't associate with people very well."

▼ "When I heard that we would have to talk about ourselves frequently, I was frightened."

▼ "A few of the things we talked about doing made me nervous and scared."

▼ "I knew most of the answers to questions directed to the class, but I didn't open my mouth once."

During weeks 3, 4, and 5, group activities examined competitive and cooperative behavior, value clarification, and defensiveness. The skills of listening and responding with understanding were emphasized. During the seminar sessions, conflict was evident, though at a manageable level. Log comments reflected the thematic content of the storming stage. As can be seen in the comments, individuals were uncomfortable about the task and relationship diversity. A more intense emotional level is evident in the comments.

STAGE 2: STORMING
Resistance and Hostility Examples

▼ "A lot of work is necessary to get an A. The problem is, it's all up to me."

▼ "Today was the first time we got in groups, and I was really uncomfortable."

▼ "When we got into groups today, no one seemed to be the leader. This wasn't good."

▼ "First time in our groups was awkward, and everyone said very little about themselves."

▼ "At first I felt a little uncomfortable in my group because I was the only one not in the nursing program."

▼ "There are two people in my group who totally ignore what the rest of us are doing and want no part of us."

▼ "Getting to know my group may take some time because we are all so different."

▼ "I was upset when we first got into our groups, but the tension eased up later on."

▼ "There seems to be a diversity of personalities among our number."

▼ "When we formed our groups, though, I think my being a male definitely kept the females from saying what they really felt."

Data from weeks 5, 6, and 7 reflect the cooperative atmosphere that had developed among the group members. Exercises in team development, group consensus, and communication were included in the group activities. Attention was given to supporting and helping others. Log comments reflected the norming theme. Students demonstrated increased self-confidence, improved communication skills, and greater awareness of others. Selected comments from their logs follow.

STAGE 3: NORMING
Communication and Cohesion Examples

▼ "Today I was able to put together the usefulness of our contracts and how great our group worked together and how we helped one other."

▼ "Everyone in the group is able to talk freely and openly with one another."

▼ "Being in the small groups made me realize that everyone is an individual with different feelings, thoughts, and emotions."

▼ In our group discussions, I was made more aware of my strengths, and this made me more confident and sure of myself."

▼ "Not only can we help ourselves, but also the other members in my group."

▼ "I had a lot of fun in class today. All of the students seem as though they really have a good sense of humor."

▼ "I could really see a difference in the way everyone in the group opens up more than we did in the beginning."

▼ "I became involved in what we were doing. Being involved really helped me in the group."

Weeks 8 and 9 provided opportunities for the productive accomplishment of assignments. Group exercises involved problem solving, evaluating, and sharing. Skills of planning, personalizing, and initiating were developed. Group members were encouraged to examine behavioral and attitudinal changes in themselves that resulted from the group interaction. Logs included numerous comments consistent with the theme of performing. Evidence of problem solving, decision making, and interdependence was apparent. Selected comments from the logs follow.

STAGE 4: PERFORMING
Problem Solving and Interdependence Examples

▼ "What we learned today in class was very interesting, and some of my friends from class and I are going to start really defending ourselves."

▼ "This class has helped me take a deeper look at myself and my actions through our small groups."

▼ "I realized that I should look at myself in depth to see how I can improve myself."

▼ "I have been relating my feelings to people a lot better. I seem to be able to get my point across more clearly."

▼ "I felt as though I knew everyone a little better, and it helped to understand them, too."

▼ "The class today, I felt, was the best yet. Everyone seemed to be open and felt easy about discussing our contracts."

▼ "Everyone is their own individual and has their own unique ways."

▼ "In our group discussions, I was made more aware of my strengths, and this made me more confident and sure of myself and gave me more courage to tackle my weaknesses."

▼ "I think it is so great we can be so open with each other."

The tenth and final week brought the seminar to a close. An opportunity was provided for group members to review and evaluate both individual and group progress. A celebration activity assisted group members in saying good-bye. Logs reflected the adjourning theme. As evidenced in the comments that follow, students were reluctant to bring closure but were proud of their achievements.

STAGE 5: ADJOURNING
Termination and Disengagement Examples

▼ "I'm going to miss these people next semester, since we will all be going our separate ways."

▼ "It's hard to leave good things."

▼ "The 10 sessions went by so quickly. It's hard to believe it's over."

▼ "I never thought I could be so involved with people so fast."

▼ "I've really enjoyed this class. It's made me so aware of things about myself that I never knew."

▼ "Because of class, I now have four new friends that know more about me than most people."

▼ "It helped me to learn to really listen to other people."

Ron summarized the findings by saying that the behavioral and attitudinal data collected from the personal logs written during the 10-week seminar on interpersonal relations, which involved small-group interaction, reflected the various stages and themes of the Tuckman group development model.

▼ BION'S BASIC ASSUMPTION GROUPS

Bion (1961) described groups as being of four types—three he called basic assumption groups and the fourth he called the work group. The basic assumption groups, called that because the assumptive name gives meaning to the prominent behavior pattern of the group, include the dependent group, the fight-flight group, and the pairing group. The dependent group focuses upon authority and the need for leadership. In the fight-flight group, conflict and attitudes of aggression and withdrawal are dominant. In the pairing group, feelings of false cohesiveness and a need for support are paramount. The work group is productive, focusing on a task and working toward accomplishing it. With their themes of dependency, conflict, cohesiveness, and performance, these groups parallel early group development ideas. All four types of groups are described in more detail in the following paragraphs. Although Bion did not describe the groups in sequential order, he noted movement from one basic assumption group to another, with the work group representing the end result.

The dependent group wants a strong leader, but members continually criticize those in leadership roles. They frequently express fears and dissatisfaction. They lack experience regarding the task of the group and are hesitant to invest in the energy for learning. They prefer traditional ways of interpreting and are slow and often reluctant to accept new ideas. No one is eager to accept responsibility for the group's task but members will complain about the lack of progress. Members are willing to be a part of the group but are unsure about how to best contribute toward its development.

The fight-flight group appears to have only two strategies for problem solving—attacking and avoiding. As a result, an atmosphere of conflict is pervasive. The needs of the individual are frequently in conflict with the needs of the group, but the group is always placed first. When the group chooses the flight mode, it abandons the individual to assure its survival. The real, legitimate work of the group is often ignored as a result of the continuous conflicts among members. A counterdependence will often develop, with group members eventually attacking the leader after having avoided that choice initially. In essence, the fight-flight group consists of unwilling members who lack understanding about how to productively work together on their assigned tasks.

The pairing group is also concerned with preserving the group. Issues of time management and relationships are critical. Anxiety and uncertainty about one's abilities and contributions to the group promote allegiances. The amount of time group members spend in discussion increases, as does the number of active participants. The group seeks cohesion. An air of hopeful expectation prevails, and an increasing faith in the leader begins to surface. Group members appear more experienced but unconfident.

The work group is characterized by being realistically task oriented. Members are focused on solving group problems and flexible in their attitudes toward leadership. They are willing to profit from their own and others' experiences. They have learned to trust the group process. The psychological structure is very powerful, and the group views itself as developing into an interdependent entity capable of solving the most challenging problems.

▼ APPLYING BION'S MODEL

As Alex reflected on his career move from a college counselor to a human resource manager, he realized that Bion's model accurately described his employees in his new job and their reactions to his leadership. The counseling to administrating job change had not been easy for him. Recalling his first year in the new position caused Alex to think more about Bion's model and the basic assumption and work groups. He began to see how his new staff fit the description of each group at different times during that time frame.

As Alex anticipated starting his new job, he prepared himself to be a strong, directive leader. He wanted to focus the entire department on the basic mission of improving service to the organization. He expected that with his openness to new suggestions and willingness to implement new ideas, this would happen quickly and current problems would be solved expediently. What he found was a highly dependent group of employees who relied on history and tradition, not dynamic leadership for direction. He made attempts at delegating and participative leadership, but the staff lacked the skills and experiences to change. Although most of the individuals appeared willing and tried to change, they soon became confused and reverted back to the old ways of doing things. Complaints soon began to surface among the employees about decreasing morale and increasing workloads. Even Alex began to get frustrated and to question his own aptitude for this new challenge.

After 3 months passed, Alex scheduled a staff retreat to examine department direction and establish specific goals for the coming year. The week before the retreat, three staff members found legitimate reasons for not attending. The atmosphere at the retreat shifted from periods of apathy to chaotic outbursts as individuals questioned every proposed change, particularly if it involved turf or ego issues. Staff members who Alex knew had effective interpersonal skills did not use them. A few individuals chose to sit quietly and participate as little as possible. As the retreat came to an end, a core group remained actively opposed to some critical goals Alex had hoped to achieve. The outcome was far from what Alex had wanted. The employees had definitely been a fight-flight group.

As the year continued, anxieties and frustrations among the staff caused increased pairings. Time management issues kept Alex busy as he attempted to coordinate the department's work in order to achieve the goals set by upper level management and imposed upon the department. By being supportive when a crisis occurred, Alex was able to begin to bring together individuals who had mutual interests and a reason to cooperate. Gradually, individuals responded with appreciation for his caring and concern. A sense of hope and an increase in willingness to be part of a team became evident. Alex recognized that his hard work and personal investment were paying off.

At the end of his first year as human resource manager, Alex was faced with making some severe budget cuts. He felt everyone in the department should be involved, as the decisions would impact each function in the unit. His past efforts began to reap rewards. The group worked. Alex began the discussion by structuring the task and the mandates pertaining to the possible solutions. Individuals responded with a realistic assessment of the parameters of the problem and a willingness to trust a group problem-solving approach. Alex was amazed. A series of sequential solutions, each predicated upon its predecessor and to be used when specific conditions occurred, was developed and supported by every member of the group. The key, however, was that everyone was involved and all had contributed to the process. There was a sense of pride and accomplishment even though each individual had lost budget monies as a result of the outcome. This was truly a work group.

▼ SCHUTZ'S THEORY OF INTERPERSONAL RELATIONS

Bill Schutz (1958) suggested a group development model focusing on interpersonal relations. Beginning with Bennis and Shepard's (1956) two-stage model of dependence and interdependence, Schutz inserted a third stage of independent assertiveness. Thus, the initial sequential stages of Schutz's model were inclusion (dependence), control (independence), and affection (interdependence). Bennis and Shepard had included a subphase in each of their stages that focused on conflict: counterdependence in phase 1 and disenchantment in phase 2. The Schutz model, called Fundamental Interpersonal Relations Orientation (FIRO), was one of the first to delineate conflict and conflict resolution (control) as a major stage in the group development process. Kaplan and Roman (1963) later suggested a similar model involving the stages of dependency, power, and intimacy. However, their model, like that of Bennis and Shepard (1956), was a linear progressive model, whereas Schutz maintained that the three stages of his model formed a cyclic pattern. In addition, as a group neared a conclusion, the pattern was reversed, moving from affection to control to inclusion issues. In an update of the theory, Schutz (1982) replaced the term *affection* with the term *openness*. Openness is more related to behavior and thus is consistent with inclusion and control; affection was more feeling oriented. He delineated five stages in his revised model: gaining inclusion, gaining control, gaining openness, giving up control, and giving up inclusion.

According to the Schutz model, gaining inclusion is the initial challenge as a group forms. Each member decides how to behave and decides whether a fit with the group is a possibility. Because fit is a matter of degree, it involves a decision about commitment to the group. How much will each person need to invest, and what are the possible outcomes that one might obtain from this investment? The main concerns of this inclusion process center on boundary issues. This stage becomes resolved when group members feel they want to be accepted and are willing to accept other members of the group.

Gaining control surfaces as an issue once members are accepted by others and begin to function as a group. Distribution of power and influence become critical variables. Leadership struggles are common, as is competition. Decisions about task direction, procedure, roles, responsibilities, and even the decision-making process itself create an atmosphere of conflict. This stage achieves resolution when individual group members take on influential roles and responsibilities but also are willing to be influenced and share responsibility with other group members.

Gaining openness occurs following the resolution of control issues. The challenge is one of emotional integration. Positive interactions increase as members begin to more readily share experiences and encourage others to reciprocate in a like manner. Group members realize they genuinely like working with one another. An emotional closeness becomes evident. This stage concludes when all group members are willing to interact in a close and personal manner with one another.

Giving up control moves the group toward team productivity. To achieve the desired interdependence, group members must focus on their individual responsibilities and trust that others will do the same. Competitive behaviors give way to collaborative ones. Synergistic problem solving becomes the norm. This stage ends when group members cease their extensive attempts to influence others and begin to encourage shared responsibilities and the empowerment of fellow group members.

Giving up inclusion occurs as a group comes to an end. Highly successful groups actually become reluctant to terminate. Group members look for ways to continue the group experience. Often ceremonies and rituals are needed to achieve meaningful closure. This stage concludes when members become willing to give up interactions with current group members in order to seek out new group experiences with new group members.

▼ APPLYING SCHUTZ'S THEORY

Irma suggested that the history of their team provided an excellent example of how Schutz's interpersonal relations theory contributes to group development theory and an understanding of team development. She traced the process that began with their early get-togethers at conferences and area workshops and continued through to their current collaborative writing project.

Initially, the foursome formed a group. The major challenge facing this group was gaining inclusion. Each member had to determine his or her willingness to include the other three. As the four friends continued to seek out and welcome one another, they were also not choosing others who might have been invited. As they became more comfortable with one another, they became less likely to bring others to their group gatherings.

The content of the gatherings soon changed from informal conversations between friends who had not seen one another for a period of time to more serious discussions of critical issues facing the profession as well as the professional development of the group members and their changing lifestyles. Once the issues involved in gaining inclusion were resolved, issues of gaining control began to surface. The group members became more active in taking leadership roles and exercising influence. Their willingness to be influenced was generally based upon their own views of the new perspectives presented. For the group, this had been a period of heightened conflict. Some of their most volatile disagreements and emotional discussions had occurred at this time. These interactions, however, provided opportunities for gaining new perspectives and clarifying personal understandings as well as for gaining increased appreciation for the viewpoints of other group members and respect for each individual as a person of worth.

As issues centered on gaining control were resolved and group members became comfortable with the influencing process and leadership roles, a concern for gaining openness became apparent. The group discussions were characterized by greater depth and personalization. Risk taking increased, and fear of rejection began to decrease. Group members genuinely liked one another and looked forward to each get-together.

The biggest and most significant challenge occurred as openness issues were resolved and the group struggled with giving up control. Trusting one another and trusting the group process required a giant leap of faith for all the members but was made somewhat easier by the simple fact that they were all doing it together. The cohesiveness of the group was a powerful factor that aided the group in resolving control issues. Irma's insight that this act of giving up control had the same criticality in a group or team as in a marriage helped the group to recognize the importance of their having achieved resolution of this issue.

It also became clear at this point that at some time in the future each member of the group would have to give up inclusion.

▼ LACOURSIERE'S LIFE CYCLE OF GROUPS

Roy Lacoursiere (1980) presented a comprehensive summary of over 200 studies of various models and theories of group development that revealed a general pattern of group developmental stages. His effort provided a historical review beginning around 1950, when organizations changed from using Frederick W. Taylor's scientific management model to using Kurt Lewin's participative management model with its emphasis on group problem solving. From this review, Lacoursiere identified five general developmental stages—orientation, dissatisfaction, resolution, production, and termination—and noted that each stage overlaps with the stages that precede and follow it. This view suggests that at any given point in the life of the group, one specific stage will dominate, but all of the stages will contribute to the functioning of the group process.

The orientation stage begins the life cycle of the group. Group members generally are willing to participate, having highly positive expectations, but are also anxious about the part they will play in the group and how they will interact with other group members and the leader. There is a dependence on authority, and initial work time is spent organizing the task and getting acquainted.

The dissatisfaction stage emerges as members' expectations do not coincide with reality. Unpleasant feelings result from the early dependence, which surface as frustration with the work of the group and anger at other group members. Frequently, that anger becomes directed at the leader as counterdependence replaces the initial dependence. Negative feelings obscure the earlier positive ones, and conflict abounds. Group members appear unwilling and unable to carry the group's work forward. Resistance is common, and there is a need for redefining and clarifying the group's direction and roles.

As group members begin to accept one another, the group enters the resolution stage. Members find numerous opportunities for independence and continued learning. They sharpen old skills and develop new ones. Their self-esteem rises, and cooperation is frequently seen. Group cohesion becomes noticeable, and work on the task increases. Group members may still, however, appear somewhat unconfident and require relationship support from the leader.

The production stage is fueled by willing and able group members who are eager to work with one another to fulfill the goals of the group. Relationships are more stable and less volatile. Success with the task increases both the positive feelings about group membership and the efficient use of work time. Pride and accomplishment are perceived as valued outcomes. Leadership is more democratic and less authoritarian, for this stage relies on interdependence for teamwork and camaraderie.

As the group experience approaches closure, each individual must deal with issues of disengaging from group membership and task completion. During the termination stage, a sadness frequently prevails, and, especially in highly successful groups, group members find it difficult to end the experience. As work on the tasks of the group decreases, the need for support increases to help the members achieve a satisfying and meaningful conclusion to the group experience.

▼ APPLYING LACOURSIERE'S MODEL

Grace's son, Tom, a college junior, had been serving as a resident assistant in one of the residence halls at his college for the past 9 months. Since the college he was attending was far from home, Grace always looked forward to his letters and telephone calls about his college experiences. As Grace reviewed Lacoursiere's model of general group developmental stages, she realized that the letters from her son throughout the past 9 months provided an appropriate case study account.

Early in the fall, as Tom began his new assignment, the theme of orientation was pervasive. He held floor meetings, visited every person on the floor, and encouraged everyone to participate in floor activities. He kept people informed and helped anyone who sought his assistance with both major and minor concerns. His letters, however, became increasingly negative as the dissatisfaction stage emerged in late October. Some of the students had not done well on the first wave of major examinations; others appeared depressed as the cold weather forced people inside. Cliques formed, and disagreements occurred daily. Some roommates were having difficulties as well. The overall feeling was that the food was bad, the courses were demanding, the weather was terrible, communication with the real world was too infrequent, and there was nothing to do but study. Few students attended floor social functions, and almost no one came to floor meetings. Some students complained to the residence hall coordinator that the noise level in the halls was getting worse and that their resident assistant was ineffective.

By semester break, however, the worst was over. The resolution stage had begun prior to final examinations. Tom had organized some study skills seminars, and with the help of a number of the floor residents he initiated a peer tutoring program. A few roommate changes were planned for the new semester, and a small group of students volunteered to help the students who would be moving onto the floor feel welcome. Only a few students planned to leave the floor, usually because of academic problems.

As the new semester began, the resolution stage gave way to the production stage. Morale was up, key support programs were in place, and almost everyone seemed willing to help one another. The months flew by despite the winter weather. Spring brought new challenges and opportunities for learning. Tom received a Residence Life Award for an alcohol awareness program he initiated on the floor, and the floor took first place in the Spring Carnival. Tom agreed to return to the resident assistant position the following year, but only after talking with the coordinator about strategies for the dissatisfaction stage.

The termination stage began following spring break and the advent of another set of final examinations. Tom, more confident than during the previous semester, helped the students through this stressful time with a support system in place that kept the atmosphere positive and upbeat. As finals came to a conclusion and the students on the floor began to disband, individuals and groups stopped to say good-bye to Tom and to one another. No one had realized how difficult leaving was going to be. Some said good-bye more than once. All wanted to keep talking about the Spring Carnival, late-night floor get-togethers, weekend activities, and even studying together for exams. The year had been fun. The students tried to plan a summer reunion but the logistics were impossible. All promised to write or call. Those who were returning to the floor the next year developed highly positive expectations, but all realized the dynamics would not be the same. No one can relive the past, and the new floor, the students knew, would create a new set of group dynamics.

▼ GROUP DEVELOPMENT DISCUSSION

Ron, Alex, Irma, and Grace met for their discussion about group development on a rainy evening. All had received and read the written summaries of the group development models and the application examples. As always, one of the team members initiated the discussion by asking the others what they had learned. Interestingly, at each meeting, a different person asked that question.

Ron pointed out that because the models described how individuals worked in groups, patterns emerged that could be viewed as stages of group development. These patterns could be characterized as being sequential, developmental, and thematic. They were sequential, he noted, in that there were specific stages that normally occurred in order. They were developmental in that each stage built on its predecessor and movement to the next stage was based on resolving the growth issues of the current stage. Finally, the stages were thematic. An overall behavioral theme described each stage as well as its task and relationship dimensions.

Alex pointed out that the time frame for the evolution of a group was situational and depended upon the amount of time the group met, the complexity of the group's task, the leadership style, and the number of group members. "Some large groups," he noted, "take months to work on complex tasks, whereas smaller groups working on a single task may progress through all of the developmental stages in a meeting of a few hours."

Irma added that more complex groups show patterns of behavior that focus on specific themes that are much like the patterns of individual growth. These groups evolve slowly over time and frequently operate much like habits. As a result, we are usually unaware of their normal and progressive development. Our awareness of their stage of development is heightened when some type of blockage prevents normal progress, especially if it results in regression. When blockage occurs, leadership intervention is helpful.

Grace suggested that leadership interventions can be used to attack fixation during a particular stage and to prevent regression. Such interventions can also be used to speed up or slow down group development in order to give added attention to task objectives, relationship demands, or individual needs. Although the storming stage is usually a time when interventions are needed to battle apathy or manage chaos, interventions are useful in all stages to promote more effective development.

Ron asked about the progress of the teams they had discussed at earlier meetings. All of those teams had appeared to be at different stages of development. He contributed an update of his strategic planning team. "When we last talked about our teams," he said, "my team was at the performing stage. It is now close to adjourning. Our work for this year is almost over, and a celebration is being planned to bring closure. All of us are very satisfied with the outcome of our work and are excited about the final vision we developed for the university's future. Now that I have knowledge about how teams conclude, I know that a few more leader interventions may be helpful. Of course, strategic planning is an ongoing process, and a number of these team members will be needed when we continue our work next year."

Irma shared her state counseling conference team results. "Our team is definitely in the performing stage," she related. "The conference is only a month away, but everything appears to be on track. Registration numbers are high, no presenters have canceled, and there is some money left in the budget for emergencies. There are still some responsibilities left, but they can be shared or delegated."

Alex talked next about his continuous quality improvement team with its goal of redesigning the company lounge. "The conflicts appeared insurmountable," he said, "but it looks as if our team is now in the norming stage. Some cooperative efforts are beginning to take shape. We did some research using focus groups and learned that employees view the lounge as an important social gathering place. Most are excited about the upcoming improvement and have offered excellent suggestions. Some are willing to help in areas where funding is short and a reliance on volunteer labor will be needed. Everyone is discussing how to get involved. Maintaining this high level of supportive behavior and providing participative opportunities are critical strategies for preparing the team for the next stage."

Grace spoke last about her parent involvement team. "What we are going through seems consistent with the theories we have discussed," she reported. Her team had an excellent beginning but was now constantly plagued with conflict. She noted, however, that "storming" seemed to be a relatively nice description. "Everyone is choosing sides," she said. "The teachers want one structure. The parents want another. Administrators who are supposed to be helpful are not, and some students don't want any parent involvement at all. They think adults just complicate things. It does appear that the chaos is better than apathy. It provides energy. I'm working at managing the conflict and bringing clarity. I've found that being assertive helps as well. Since all teams have this experience and continue to grow and develop, what we're going through must be normal. I'm hopeful that norming will occur soon."

Irma noted that all of them had used the Tuckman terminology in their recent reports. Ron thought that since he had gone first, others simply followed his lead. Alex, however, felt strongly that because Tuckman's terms rhyme, they are easier to remember and use. Grace agreed, and she added that Tuckman's use of behavioral descriptions that have both task and relationship components was also a plus.

Alex distributed a handout that summarized the four models of group development they had researched. This handout is presented as Table 2.1. All appreciated his effort. The team members spent the final minutes of their discussion selecting a topic for their next meeting. All agreed with Grace, who made a dramatic plea to learn more about conflict and the nature of change.

TABLE 2.1 *Stages of Group Development*

	Theories/Models			
Stages	Tuckman (1965, 1977)	Bion (1961)	Schutz (1958, 1982)	Lacoursiere (1980)
1	Forming: Orientation, dependence	Dependency or pairing	Gaining inclusion	Orientation
2	Storming: Resistance, hostility	Fight/flight	Gaining control	Dissatisfaction
3	Norming: Communication, cohesion	Pairing or dependency	Gaining openness	Resolution
4	Performing: Problem solving, interdependence	Work	Giving up control	Production
5	Adjourning: Termination, disengagement		Giving up inclusion	Termination

Change
and Conflict

*Anxiety in human life is what
squeaking and grinding are in
machinery that is not oiled. In life,
trust is the oil.*

—Henry Ward Beecher

*G*race, Alex, Irma, and Ron finally met again after having to postpone their get-together twice because of summer vacations. The irony, of course, was that the discussion topic was change and conflict. All agreed that increases in the amount of change produce increased conflict. Grace added that the rapidity of change has the same effect. Alex asked if change was a choice, as he typically felt compelled to change. He noted that the act of his not choosing to make changes usually resulted in others making those choices for him. Ron suggested that change was a given and that the real choice was in how and when to influence the change process. Irma noted that the change process in group and team development frequently involved a conflict stage and that when conflict issues were skipped over, the group would eventually regress backward and engage those issues, sometimes more than once. Alex pointed out that within the group and team context, conflict, like change, is a naturally occurring process. In fact, it appears to be an essential component to the growth and development of a group or team.

Ron introduced the idea that if conflict is essential to growth, it should be viewed as positive with its extremes viewed as negative. He noted that too much conflict results in chaos and the absence of conflict encourages apathy. Grace added that managing conflict is therefore an important skill for influencing change. "So is managing emotions," Irma said, "since conflict is frequently accompanied by anxiety and tension." Alex stated that conflict also increases energy and expressed a preference for chaotic groups over apathetic ones. "At least, with the former, you have the energy for change," he said. All began to view understanding conflict as an important insight for team development. They reached the conclusion that it was important to trust the group development process and understand that the anxiety and tension of natural conflict provides the energy for continued growth. They noted, too, that leadership interventions may be needed for effective conflict management.

Each had done extensive research and writing given the extra time they had as a result of postponed meetings. Alex had written about the nature of conflict. Irma had chosen the causes of conflict. Grace had examined conflict and leadership. Ron had looked at managing change.

▼ THE NATURE OF CONFLICT

The storming stage of group development involves a movement toward conflict. It follows the movement toward awareness in the forming stage. Group members who were originally eager and willing to participate may now be exhibiting signs of resistance and hostility. Their inexperience compounds the situation. As member interactions and task involvement increase, so do possibilities for conflict (Kormanski, 1982).

Conflict in this context is a naturally occurring behavior pattern and an essential stage in the growth and development of the group. Thus, it is a positive phenomenon and a prerequisite for group growth. Just as algebra and trigonometry are prerequisites for calculus, healthy conflict is necessary for promoting group development.

Individual development follows a similar pattern. One grows and matures more quickly during periods of personal conflict. A change in schools, a move to a new neighborhood, the loss of a good friend, a family divorce or separation, a change in job status, or the death of someone close—each, in its own unique way, challenges the individual to react in a more responsible manner, to take charge of the situation, to keep control of his or her emotions, to act in an initiatory and decisive way. Conflict frequently brings out the best in each of us as long as we are developmentally ready for the challenge.

As noted earlier, the key to resolving the issues of the storming stage is to manage conflict, not eliminate it. Unmanaged conflict becomes chaos that will create a barrier to the further development of the group. The absence of conflict encourages apathy, which may be worse than chaos because it results in a lack of energy with which to work. Effective leaders are adept at introducing conflict into apathetic groups to increase the energy for change and at reframing chaotic groups to create a focused direction that all members can follow.

Dana (1984) suggested that group conflict can result in a number of costs that take a toll on both the people and the finances of today's organizations. The costs include wasted management time; reduced decision quality; loss of skilled employees; restructuring; employee sabotage; lowered motivation; lost work time; and health costs. Indeed, current trends in business and industry may be increasing the level of these costs. The increasing diversity of the workforce is bringing more value, attitude, and behavioral differences into the workplace. Participative management is giving more individuals supervisory responsibilities. With these changes, conflict is increasing.

Yet conflict is necessary for change. The use of teams and task forces is providing a natural setting for the group development process to unfold. With this process comes the storming stage and the potential for continued growth.

Trends in educational institutions follow those in business and industry. The challenge of developing a more skillful and adaptable workforce rests on the abilities of our schools to graduate students with the ability to learn. The skills needed in the global marketplace mostly involve communications, computers, and interpersonal relations, including skills in conflict management. We are at the beginning of the age of information, and creating learning organizations is fast becoming the preferred survival strategy.

Peters (1987) encouraged thriving on chaos and noted that the core paradox that leaders at all levels must face is the need to foster internal stability in order to encourage change. He stressed a view of leadership that establishes direction by developing an inspiring vision, managing by example, and practicing visible management; that empowers people by increased listening, deferring to the front line, delegating, reducing bureaucracy, and increasing horizontal management; and that embraces the process of change. In essence, success will come to those who thrive on chaos and learn how to manage conflict effectively.

Peters (1987) posited nine tips for simultaneously creating stability and instability:

▼ Be out and about (management by walking around).
▼ Demand empiricism (have everybody evaluate everything).
▼ Listen (institute listening forums and encourage sharing).
▼ Laud failure (test fast, fail fast, adjust fast).
▼ Proclaim speedy horizontal action taking (involve multiple functions).
▼ Define common denominators (make successful group efforts visible).
▼ Let customers teach (learn from those you serve).

▼ Make the workplace fun (take pleasure in successes and failure alike).

▼ Promote those who deal best with paradox (reward change).

In addition, he suggested that leaders organize as much as possible around teams and that the self-managing team should become the basic organizational building block. Understanding group development theory is critical for putting these ideas into practice.

Although the storming stage is the expected venue for conflict, it will occur in other stages as well. Certainly, some conflict is involved in getting started and in resolving dependency issues during the forming stage. It occurs in the norming stage as procedures and standards are developed and communication is emphasized. The interdependence of the problem-solving, performing stage is not without conflict. Finally, closing down projects and groups creates some conflict during the adjourning stage.

▼ THE CAUSES OF CONFLICT

As a group gets oriented and dependency upon the leader decreases, an atmosphere of counterdependency begins to surface (Bennis & Shepard, 1956). Conflict will not always be loud and obvious with illogical ideas and irrational emotions taking center stage. Frequently, it will present itself as differences of opinions, as members presenting a variety of alternatives or choices, or as members suggesting different opportunities for taking action. All of these offer positive possibilities. Sometimes conflict will be subtle, quiet, and hardly noticeable. Identifying conflict of this type involves observing nonverbal behavior, communication patterns, and unmet human needs. If left unattended, such conflict will smolder and eventually create feelings of resentment and a behavior pattern best described as "good old-fashioned" stubbornness.

Conflicts may be classified as involving behaviors, attitudes, or values. Behavioral conflicts have been described as approach-approach, avoidance-avoidance, or approach-avoidance in reference to a specific goal (Lewin, 1951). The approach-approach conflict involves two or more positive goals. Only one of the goals is attainable at a given point in time, as movement toward it is movement away from the other goal(s). The choice of a college major, a marriage partner, a vacation site, or a movie involves this type of conflict.

The avoidance-avoidance conflict represents the opposite dilemma. One must choose among a number of negative outcomes. Taking the lesser of two evils is the end result. The prospective employee who has to choose an entry-level job from among several in the company when he or she really wants a higher level position and the teenager who must choose among several punishment options for staying out too late are faced with this type of conflict.

The approach-avoidance conflict occurs when choices contain both positive and negative components. The single approach-avoidance conflict involves deciding whether to approach a goal with a positive-negative mixture; the double approach-avoidance conflict involves more than one mixture choice. Deciding whether to eat at one's first choice of restaurants when it will be necessary to stand in line for an hour is an example of the former; deciding on a job offer or college to attend is an example of the latter.

Attitude conflicts occur between individuals with different personalities and may involve the way in which events are perceived and are evaluated. Such differences lead to misinterpretations, which may result in defensiveness, misunderstandings, or feelings of being rejected, devalued, or stereotyped. These added complications increase the complexity of the situation and heighten the emotional climate within which the conflict occurs. Issues of control and influence are frequently central to personality conflicts.

Value conflicts are more deeply rooted than other types of conflicts and often come to light in decisions about lifestyle and work style. Our values are not altered as easily or as quickly as are our attitudes or behaviors. In fact, core values that are formed in childhood are quite resistant to change and persist into our adult life. Making a choice between a value that has a negative connotation and one with a positive connotation is relatively easy. Being honest versus dishonest, acting lazy versus being ambitious, and feeling sincere versus feeling insincere are typical examples. Selecting among a number of positive values in a given situation is much more difficult. Should one choose honesty, ambitiousness, or sincerity? We have already chosen most of our values by the time we leave childhood. The real challenge is in prioritizing our values and in dealing with the conflict that comes when we interact with other individuals who hold similar values to ours but have prioritized them in a different manner. In addition, changing situations can create changes in the prioritization of a value set.

▼ CONFLICT AND LEADERSHIP

Conflict and leadership are inseparable (Burns, 1978). As conflict increases, the need for effective leadership increases (Kormanski, 1982). Effective leadership within conflict situations mandates both knowledge of and skill in conflict management techniques. The group leader should acknowledge conflict and share the positive benefits that can be derived from it.

Much of leadership involves influencing and controlling change. As our environment becomes more complex and involves increased interpersonal interactions, individual effort has less impact (Kormanski & Mozenter, 1987). Group effort is fast becoming the preferred strategy for managing change and teamwork the preferred process. Both rely heavily on group development theory as a basis upon which to build implementation efforts. Education can learn from business and vice versa. Seeing similar problems in a different setting will often provide the necessary perspective for developing innovative solutions.

Ohme (1977) offered a law of institutional change that suggests that it is not the merit of the plan but the right combination of leadership and member involvement that determines successful outcomes. Such a working relationship is best accomplished through participative management, but only after group members have had some appropriate experience and training. When an organization is willing to make the investment necessary to provide these opportunities to their employees, a new atmosphere surrounding the workplace is possible. As stated by Rosebeth Moss Kanter (1983), "After years of telling corporate citizens to trust the system, many organizations must relearn instead to trust their people" (p. 18).

Day and Roth (1980) offered the following seven methodological assumptions for effectively managing change within an organization:

▼ starting at points of readiness;
▼ using a bottom-up, top-down approach;
▼ making creative use of bureaucracy;
▼ viewing crisis as opportunity;
▼ having a clear image of ideal change;
▼ espousing the attitude of doing things better, not perfectly; and
▼ having a "we can muddle through" philosophy.

Strategies that have proven useful as interventions include:

▼ using ad hoc task forces;
▼ mixing mandated change with creative input;
▼ using crisis to further change;
▼ scanning the system for small trouble spots;
▼ maintaining a holistic policy;
▼ conceptualizing major efforts as projects; and
▼ involving everyone in the change process.

People resist change only when it is imposed (Burke & Church, 1992). Highly involving those who are most affected by the change in the planning process reduces resistance and improves the implementation of the plan (Bennis, 1990). Commitment and ownership are powerful sources of motivation. Ownership in team projects demands a high level of maturity from everyone involved (DePree, 1989).

Leadership can be transactional or transformational. Transactional leadership manages conflict while transformational leadership builds both morale and maturity. The need for both is obvious. The former addresses the challenges of the present; the latter influences the future. DePree (1992) has suggested that we too often focus only on what we need to do and neglect what we need to be.

Visioning and empowerment are critical skills for leaders (Block, 1987). Both represent higher level motivation needs for individuals and groups. Providing opportunities for individuals and groups to fulfill these needs is a major task of leadership (Kormanski, 1994). Effective leaders use the change process and conflict as opportunity for both individual and group development. Both task accomplishment and quality relationships are important goals. Visioning provides the direction and meaning. Empowerment leads to a motivated group of achievers.

The principles of transactional and transformational leadership are reflected in the following description of a seminar for a group of small business owners interested in initiating strategic planning in their companies. Meeting monthly, this group was composed of owners of a variety of community firms involved in communications, food service, engineering, transportation, health care, consulting, scientific research, personnel, and real estate. They quickly identified the rapidity of change in the workplace as a critical concern that resulted in frequent conflicts.

The consensus viewpoint was that as the speed and intensity of change increased, the following dynamics were evident for their employees:

▼ They became less competent, less confident, and more uncomfortable.
▼ They were at different readiness levels to handle changes.
▼ They did not think they had adequate resources.
▼ They focused upon what they would have to give up.
▼ They reacted with limited creativity and reduced risk taking.
▼ They gradually increased their resistance and frustration to anything new.
▼ They acted in a reactionary manner rather than looking to the future.
▼ They could handle only so much change at one time.
▼ They lacked insight and understanding of change dynamics.
▼ They reverted to previous behavior patterns when the pressure to change was reduced.

The major conflict for the owners was in balancing attention to the current crisis and attention to the future of the business. Furthermore, the business owners did not see themselves as having time to do both.

Therefore, they postponed the latter until they could gain control of the former. Before this group began to meet they rarely gave any substantial time or effort to future planning.

The need for strategic planning and employee involvement in the process became apparent to the owners as the seminar presenters described how successful organizations were profiting from this endeavor. The owners were still concerned, however, that the small size of their businesses and the low motivation level of their few employees were hindrances.

They would need both transactional and transformational leadership to successfully implement strategic planning. Employee involvement would be essential. Creating and sharing a vision would be critical. The use of the current conflict as an opportunity for empowering employees and fostering organizational growth was seen as a major goal. The following strategies were developed to achieve this desired outcome:

▼ Publicly commit to the strategic planning process.
▼ Build a small but diverse strategic planning team.
▼ Create opportunities for all members of the organization to participate by using surveys, focus groups, forums, training events, regular meetings, and interviews to gather data.
▼ Demonstrate how mission, values, and vision are being used in the organization.
▼ Establish three to five strategic goals along with related strategies and measurable objectives (critical success indicators).
▼ Measure progress regularly and publish results.
▼ Make sure the strategic plan is data driven.
▼ Provide regular feedback and updates about the strategic planning process.
▼ Reward participation and contributions.
▼ Model strategic thinking and transformational leadership qualities.

The final and most challenging strategy was to establish a regular meeting time for the strategic planning team.

▼ MANAGING CHANGE

The choice by team leaders to influence change is a key component of group growth and development. Team leaders foster change by providing direction and maintaining commitment among the members. Thinking strategically enhances the process of managing change by encouraging a balance between attention to the present (operational issues) and focus on the future (strategic issues).

To complicate matters, issues are not either/or entities but fall somewhere along the continuum between being operational and being strategic. Furthermore, issues are not static; they are typically moving in a developmental direction (from strategic to operational). Effective leaders and teams that function successfully as change agents are able to differentiate and manage multiple issues of change within their organization.

Strategic planning is a viable method for managing change in organizations. It is used to help those in leadership roles think and act more decisively about the organization's future. Thus, the most important desired outcome of this critical intervention is to create strategic planners, not simply to create a strategic plan. Thinking strategically is the essential process (Kormanski, 1994). The plan that is developed represents the outcome of that process.

Although the paradigm once existed that permanent solutions could be developed for temporary problems, that paradigm has been changed radically (Kormanski, 1994; Schein, 1985). Indeed, Peter Senge (1990) has suggested that the solutions of yesterday are frequently the problems of today. The current belief is that there are permanent problems in need of temporary solutions. With time, temporary solutions lose their effectiveness and begin to contribute to the problem. A new temporary solution is required that is more appropriate for the problem's new characteristics.

The following example illustrates this paradigm shift. When personal computers were introduced into a worksite to increase employee efficiency and effectiveness, the unit head viewed the computers as a permanent solution to the temporary problem of work overload and the resultant stress on employees. However, the computers necessitated set-up time, training, continuous upgrades, and more training. The

pany hierarchy increased work standards using the rationale that technology had been improved and expressed a need for a return on investment of costs. In addition, the everyday challenges of the new technology created a new set of problems that added stress to the employees and required assigning one of them, who had already developed some computer skills, to the function of coaching the others. This responsibility took time away from aspects of her regular job, and others had to be assigned to help in those areas. Thus, more temporary solutions were needed to address what is best considered a permanent problem—work overload and employee stress—for it will surface again when the new solutions wear out.

Another example of this paradigm shift concerns the job search following educational graduation. In the past, the job search was viewed as a temporary problem for many; the initial job was a permanent solution. Today, increases in company downsizing, in small business ownership, in part-time employment, in working at home, and related career dynamics have resulted in the job search being viewed as a permanent problem, even for those who have a job (Barker, 1992). Job and career changes are increasing in number both within and between organizations, as are the number of individuals who choose to start their own businesses. Job search strategies have become temporary solutions for a permanent problem.

Strategic thinking encourages the development of multiple solutions that can be stacked in a timeline much like commercial airplanes are arranged for takeoff and landing at major airports. As one solution loses its impact, the next one is adapted and applied. This process is enhanced by a team approach involving a variety of perspectives from creative individuals who can develop numerous integrative solutions.

Following planning, action must occur. Thus, for the effective leader, decision making must include action. Too often the heightened enthusiasm and attention to detail that characterize the planning phase of a project are lost when implementation begins. This is particularly true when planners delegate plans to implementers who have had limited involvement in the planning.

Since no one can do everything at once, effective leaders prioritize items based on needs and resources. They are not paralyzed by being overwhelmed with multiple demands for action. Decisive action by leaders also involves an element of risk taking. David McClelland (1961) described achievement-motivated individuals as those who take moderate risks that result in a 40–60% chance of success. A corollary to moderate risk taking is the willingness by superiors to accept modest failures and to view failure as a valuable learning experience. Strategic thinking encourages leaders to use both successful and unsuccessful action to promote learning.

No one can predict the future, but effective leaders can influence it. The skill of visioning involves building an ideal scenario for the organization at some point in the future. Whereas a mission is fairly stable over time, a vision is in a constant state of change. The vision becomes more clear, concrete, and specific as one moves from the present into the future. A hiker climbing a series of mountains provides an appropriate analogy. As the hiker climbs the first mountain in the chain, she makes decisions regarding her specific pathway and use of energy. A map provides some clues. As she ascends each other mountain in the chain, she adds data to her hiking experience that influences the continuous building of her vision of what she hopes to achieve as she hikes along.

Some of the most difficult but important decisions are made today but will not impact the organization until tomorrow. These decisions are major building blocks for the future scenario. Senge (1990) noted that even though such changes may be small, they can produce big results. Further, those areas of the highest leverage may often be the least obvious. Strategic thinking requires a visionary perspective that involves taking risks that are challenging and realistic. It provides direction and motivation.

Visionary champions are essential if the vision is to be carried throughout the organization. Maslow's (1971) description of self-actualized people can be summarized as those who live their values. True champions of strategic thinking become the vision. They are what they believe. These individuals position themselves where the strategic planning action is and continuously demonstrate the congruency among values, attitudes, and behaviors.

When asked about his phenomenal success as a hockey player, Wayne Gretsky (1993) responded that his objective is to skate to where the puck will be. Like many exceptional athletes, he arrives before the action begins and is able to secure a position of leverage and influence. Strategic thinking by the organizational leadership has the potential to give the organization this same advantage. Teams that can apply the concepts of strategic thinking and implement visions are powerful change agents.

▼ MORE GROUP DEVELOPMENT DISCUSSION

Grace, Alex, Irma, and Ron discussed how conflict appeared to affect their individual groups. Grace noted that conflict had been crucial to the development of all of their teams. Her parent involvement team appeared to be finally managing its conflict. Even the students had become active. Volunteer parent groups were now participating in a variety of programs throughout the school district. Grace found that she still had to provide a lot of support and encouragement. A few minor conflicts still surfaced but were quickly managed. Grace felt more confident about her own understanding of group dynamics and skills as a team facilitator.

Alex spoke about his continuous quality improvement team and how their project was almost completed. He was delegating the few remaining tasks and had already begun to plan a celebration activity. Organizational management had not only praised the quality of the project but were extremely pleased with the working relationships among Alex's staff. He was convinced that the early conflicts were what brought the team together and created a sense of belonging and cohesion.

Irma reported on her state counseling conference. It had been both a professional and a financial success. Like Alex, she saw the early conflicts as building commitment and clarity among the team members. A recent party celebrated the final accounting report, which had resulted in an excellent profit for the state counseling association.

Ron reiterated that change and conflict were constantly intertwined and that managing conflict was a major contributor to influencing change. The disagreements concerning prioritizing issues, setting realistic goals, and how to best measure progress were particularly emotional and required an extended period of time to resolve. He asked the other team members what each of them did, specifically, to manage conflicts in their individual teams. Was there a strategy that worked best?

Grace responded to Ron's question about a preferred strategy for managing conflict by describing her use of authority with her parent involvement team. With so many team members and so little time, she instituted democratic voting as a means of determining the majority opinion. At times, the team also used expert authority, and when Grace had to make an important decision between meetings she used her personal authority.

Alex's favorite strategy was compromise. His continuous quality improvement team frequently had limited resources, and compromise allowed everyone to win a little. He admitted to enjoying the bargaining process that created the final outcome. Compromise was not the only strategy used for managing change, but for Alex it was the most exciting.

Irma's concern for keeping everyone happy resulted in her using consensus most of the time. Her state counseling conference committee was small, and seeking agreement from all was essential. This integrative approach took time but provided a highly supportive climate.

Ron noted that his strategic planning team had used all of these strategies plus a few more. None was a strong favorite of his, but the decision to use each was based upon situational variables. "At times," he said, "suppression of one's own preference and willingness to go along with another choice made sense; at other times, simply withdrawing from the conflict seemed to work best."

The team members reached a consensus by agreeing that situational variables were critical, and each volunteered to investigate one of the strategies. The results were to be mailed to each member prior to the next meeting. Grace, Alex, and Irma choose their favorite strategies, which were authority, compromise, and consensus. Ron consented to examine suppression and withdrawal as strategies. Their summaries follow.

▼ AUTHORITY AS A STRATEGY

The use of authority involves utilizing power to influence attitudes, behavior, or both. Basic sources of power include the ability to reward and punish (reward and coercive powers); official regulations, contracts, and positions (legitimate power); competence (expert power); personality (referent power); relationships (connective power); and knowledge (information power). These seven sources are often divided into the categories of position power and personal power (Machiavelli, 1952). Position power includes the reward, coercive, legitimate, and connective types; personal power consists of the referent, informational, and expert types (French & Raven, 1959; Hersey, Blanchard, & Natemeyer, 1979).

People often think of authority as being held by one individual or by a small group. Democratic voting, however, is nothing less than the authority of the majority. Authority is used most advantageously in crisis situations with short time constraints and in situations in which the involved parties are unable to find common areas of agreement (Kormanski, 1982). Authority often becomes the preferred choice when other techniques do not resolve the conflict or when others are incompetent. It is also a useful strategy when an unpopular decision needs to be made and may be required when decisions that are critical to the survival of the organization are involved. The major disadvantage of authority is that it creates win-lose situations, and losers do not work as hard as winners to implement the chosen alternative. In addition, the use of authority can foster the growth of resentment and feelings of powerlessness if used too frequently. It also promotes dependency. Arbitration is a typical example of the use of authority. Some other examples follow.

Seventy percent of the students in a career guidance class had been completing their weekly assignments 1 to 2 days late. The instructor, Mark, stressed the importance of completing assignments on time. Now, 40% of the assignments were coming in late. An authority strategy would be appropriate. Mark had set a specific standard, but many of the students were not following through in a competent manner. A decision to deduct points would be appropriate.

The committee appointed to arrange a retirement dinner for an unpopular but loyal employee had not competed its task by the set deadline. The chairperson and one of the three members of the committee were currently on vacation, leaving another committee member,

Jane, in charge. Even though this event would likely be unpopular, Jane's commitment to the system compelled her to make an authoritative intervention to meet the deadline and follow through with the event.

As a result of a recent transfer and the notification that the transferee's previous position would not be filled, Stan needed to realign work responsibilities in the guidance department. An organizational value stressed attention to student needs, and Stan wanted to avoid gaps of service. No one on his staff wanted the added duties or the responsibility for the decision of who should acquire these duties. Stan used his authority, after collecting input from each staff person, to quickly create a realignment of duties. He stressed to those involved the crucial nature and timing of the decision to ensure organizational survival.

The use of authority always requires follow-up monitoring by leadership. Leaders must review reactions by losers, the presence of dependency behaviors, and any increases in emotions to assess their impact and the need for additional leadership interventions. The wise use of power can be very helpful in such instances. Being able to balance concern for the individual and concern for the organization as well as make decisions that are fair, logical, and consider the impact on all people involved is a challenge for any leader.

▼ COMPROMISE AS A STRATEGY

The use of compromise involves each individual or group giving up a little and obtaining some of what it wants to achieve resolution of the conflict. This strategy ensures that everyone wins. The creation of win-win sets fosters cooperative behavior and promotes collaborative learning among team members. Individuals are encouraged to identify preferences and build solutions on the basis of combinations of selected priorities. Occurrences of win-lose sets are reduced, and lose-lose sets are eliminated (Kormanski, 1982).

The use of compromise behavior reflects a political model of group interaction and leadership (Baldridge, 1971). Conflicting groups realize that when there are limitations of time, personnel, or materials, solutions must be constructed that provide for equal and just distribution of the limited commodities. In groups, individuals learn to collaborate together and be satisfied with achieving team goals instead of personal goals. Leaders and facilitators must monitor both individual and group demands to ensure that wants are realistic and not increased in anticipation of a compromise solution.

One disadvantage to this approach is that because the chosen solution is not necessarily the best or second best choice but the only one for which there was agreement, the eventual action could be weak or ineffective. Another disadvantage is that those in conflict may begin to inflate their wants and demands in future situations. The advantages are that this approach can be used to delay or forgo win-lose situations; it is useful when the power between parties is equal; and it is extremely effective in situations in which resources are limited (Kormanski, 1982). Negotiation is typically involved in compromise; however, a third party is often needed to direct the process. Examples of compromise follow.

Two employees have requested the same 2-week vacation period. They are the only employees trained to carry out an essential task. Some type of compromise is needed. Possible solutions where each employee would win a little include each employee selecting one of the two weeks and the employees alternating the 2-week period each year.

Two groups of support staff have identified a number of undesirable tasks they are currently performing that they think the other group should be performing. The groups, which have equal power, continue to complain about having to complete the tasks themselves. A compromise strategy would delineate the task responsibilities and standards for each group. With such a strategy, the undesirable tasks could be divided in a fair and just manner.

Budget requests for all departments in an institution had to be cut for the past 2 years. Preparation for this year's budget has begun, and rumors are flying that some departments are inflating their needs in order to acquire more financial resources. A compromise strategy that limits the amount or the percentage of increase over the current year's budget request would be in order.

In all of these examples, compromise was used to create win-win sets when resources were limited and power was equal. Constant vigilance is required, however, to combat inflation attempts as well as to ascertain if the selected alternative is strong enough to be effective.

Sometimes compromises result in the weakest choice because of the need to reach agreement. As has been noted, a third party is often needed to conduct the negotiations.

▼ CONSENSUS AS A STRATEGY

The consensus approach is based on the idea of seeking a solution with which everyone can live. Each individual involved in the conflict is encouraged to take part in problem solving—to reexamine the situation, identify points of agreement, and help come up with new alternatives. The conflicting parties should be able to accept group decisions on the basis of logic and feasibility (Hall, 1971). Although complete unanimity is preferred, total consensus is difficult to reach and may not always be achieved.

Weisbord (1992) advocated seeking common ground, a strategy similar to consensus. In this strategy the team members identify consensus possibilities and specific topics for which consensus is currently not possible. The team then seeks consensus for the topics for which agreement is possible and agrees to postpone work on those topics for which consensus is not possible until a later time. The rapidity of change suggests that enough significant variables will be altered at some point in the future that consensus may eventually be achieved for topics that are presently unresolvable.

Consensus seeking is a popular technique of group leaders. This integrative technique is frequently chosen to teach and develop channels for open communication and to build cohesiveness and unity within the group. Additional techniques that are integrative in nature include brainstorming, the nominal group process, force field analysis, role-playing, and related problem-solving methods (Kormanski, 1982).

A disadvantage to integration is that it is time consuming. In addition, the conflicting individuals may be unwilling to put team or organizational goals before personal goals. The advantages of this approach include the identification of new and creative solutions as well as the building of team cohesiveness and commitment. Consensus, like compromise, is a way to produce a win-win outcome. Mediation is a typical example of consensus. Other examples follow.

At a recent staff meeting, two individuals disagreed over how written reports should be filed. One individual thought each department should maintain its own file for easy access. The other individual thought that by maintaining a central file, expenses could be reduced and all materials would be kept together. A consensus strategy could be used to help the individuals apply problem solving to their obvious impasse. The focus would be on creating new alternatives to the current dilemma that both individuals could accept.

A group representing 40% of the staff of an organization requested that during the summer, the office be opened an hour early so that employees could have more evening time at home. They were certain others would support their idea. One employee knew for sure that at least one department would not support the idea and mentioned that fact. A vote was suggested. Integration, however, would be a better strategy. Voting results in two factions, winners and losers, and losers do not work as diligently as winners to implement the voted-upon decision. Furthermore, if the losing faction is substantial (30% or more), it can erode morale and commitment to current and future goals.

In another organization, it had become obvious that the department copy machine was being used for a variety of personal reasons including copying obscene jokes. As each week passed, the behavior increased and was noticeable by staff and clients. A consensus strategy confronted the situation and promoted open communication. Trust was imperative. With today's concern for organizational values, public image, and customer service, the behavior employees exhibit during the workday communicates the degree of professionalism represented by a particular office or department. To manage conflict involving employee behavior, group commitment is needed. In the current scenario, the leader could not provide the time that would be needed for authoritative supervision; compromises were not acceptable; the problem behavior was increasing, thus ruling out suppression; and the matter was too important for withdrawal to be a possibility. All department members needed to be involved in establishing a policy and monitoring its implementation. Consensus would be the preferred strategy.

In all of these examples the emphasis was upon including those involved in the conflict in the problem-solving process. The strategy breaks down when there is not enough time for the process to be completed. Hidden agendas and placing personal goals above organizational goals hinder the process. Finally, because consensus is a communicative strategy that encourages flexibility and creativity, it does not work with dull, rigid people.

▼ SUPPRESSION AS A STRATEGY

The suppression strategy consists of the leader or facilitator giving the conflict issue less attention, thus creating a climate that does not feed the growth of the conflict. Emotions are kept under control by an active dialogue that emphasizes empathic understanding. The use of suppression allows the facilitator time to build a more supportive climate before using consensus, compromise, or authority interventions. This strategy is commonly used for issues that are beyond the influence of the team as well as for those of lesser importance that may soon be forgotten. A budget decision based upon federal regulations is an example of the former; the decision to have employees sit alphabetically at staff meetings to ensure equal participation is an example of the latter.

Sometimes, the relationship with the team member involved in a conflict issue is more important than the issue. The relationship factor takes priority over the task. Because of friendship, respect, esteem, trust, or recognized competence, the conflict issue receives minimal concern. A group leader makes a decision to strengthen the self-concept of the individual rather than ensure the completion of a specific task. For similar reasons, we often choose to engage in a disliked activity because a friend wants our help (Kormanski, 1982).

Suppression is most effective when the issue is beyond the control of the group, an emotional cooling down period is needed, or an important relationship is involved in the conflict. The disadvantages to using this strategy include the fact that the conflict issue may continue to smolder and may erupt later. In addition, by using suppression frequently, one could be viewed as being weak and giving in to the opposition. The following are examples of the suppression strategy.

Two complaints have appeared in the suggestion box regarding gossip and rumor-spreading behavior by school staff. Both complaints were signed and expressed concern for the feelings of others. Talking with the individuals who wrote the complaints and using a suppression strategy would be most appropriate. This strategy would provide an opportunity to put emotions into perspective and to assess how widespread the issue is.

Few of the staff of a Midwest organization attended the office's Fourth of July picnic at Sam's house last year. However, Sam, who has been with the organization for 25 years, asked if he could plan and host the picnic again this year. A few employees have already suggested that the event be canceled. Since attendance is not mandatory and individuals are not expected to attend, suppression would be an appropriate strategy. Sam is a loyal employee and enjoys hosting this event. For the office manager, the issue is not as important as the relationship. Even though she does not see a lot of value in the affair, she decides to support Sam in his efforts. In addition, she will probably attend what will likely be a very dull picnic because she likes Sam. She might even offer him a few suggestions to liven up this year's picnic.

Both of these situations involve important relationships and/or issues that do not appear significant but could become so quickly. The suppression strategy allows the leader to be part of the issue and gives the leader access to information. Because the leader is not taking direct action, however, use of this strategy may cause him or her to appear to be weak and ineffective.

▼ WITHDRAWAL AS A STRATEGY

This strategy involves the team leader remaining at a distance or actually moving away from the conflict. He or she postpones involvement and selects a passive position. By not pushing leader involvement, the individual allows conflicts to be resolved naturally by the team members. Use of this strategy reduces the possibility of excessive leader influence. The leader can use this time of noninvolvement for observation and data collection. By postponing an intervention, the leader lessens his or her impulse to join one of the conflicting sides.

Situations most appropriate for withdrawal include those in which critical information is lacking, the leader is powerless, the issue is unimportant, others are more competent at resolving the issue than the leader is, and the leader does not wish to choose sides. There must be adequate time to implement this strategy. In addition to the time needed for the group members to resolve the conflict, there must be time for the leader to implement one of the other strategies should withdrawal not prove effective (Kormanski, 1982). The disadvantages of this approach are that it cannot be used in a crisis situation; the leader gives up his or her opportunity for legitimate action, may be perceived as a failure, and loses his or her access to firsthand information; and important conflicts may grow into large, serious ones. The examples that follow illustrate the withdrawal strategy.

A heated argument in the lounge has resulted in damage to the coffee machine. Both parties involved blame each other. No witnesses have volunteered additional information. The coffee machine was purchased by volunteer contributions from the staff. Withdrawal would be an appropriate strategy. From a leadership perspective, the leader is missing critical information and would want to avoid choosing sides.

Two departments have requested budget increases for supplies and ask for the department head, Maria, to support them. A finance officer, not Maria, will make the decision. Maria is aware that increasing funds for one group will result in decreases in funds for all others, as the total budget figure for supplies is set. Using the withdrawal strategy would be Maria's best choice. She does not have the power to make the budget decision, and it is to her advantage to not choose sides.

In both of these situations, the leader does not have problem ownership, and neither situation presents a dire crisis. The leader may, however, be perceived as a failure for not choosing to take action, and the issues could grow into more serious situations. If withdrawal does not work, the leader could reenter the conflict and implement a different strategy at some future time.

▼ DISCUSSION OF CONFLICT STRATEGIES

Irma, Ron, Grace, and Alex engaged in a lively and insightful discussion about the conflict management strategies the team members had summarized. Irma agreed to put their ideas into written form, adding some appropriate references. Her summary concludes this chapter.

Ron suggested that since effective leadership was mentioned so frequently in their discussion of conflict and change, this might be an appropriate topic for the next team meeting. Grace agreed to coordinate the topic selection, and Alex volunteered to secure a meeting facility. Irma commented on how easily and with minimal conflict the team had made these arrangements.

▼ CHOOSING A STRATEGY: A SUMMARY

The strategics for conflict management can be arranged in a hierarchy with authority at the lowest and most powerful level followed by compromise, consensus, suppression, and withdrawal. This hierarchy of conflict management strategies and a set of contingencies for choosing an appropriate strategy for a specific conflict are presented in Table 3.1. These contingency guidelines provide assessment criteria for conducting a situational analysis.

The leader begins by assessing the situation in which the conflict is occurring. The ability to identify key parameters and priorities is critical to the leadership role. Because each strategy has both advantages and disadvantages, selection is situational. Emphasis should be given to such situational variables as the task to be accomplished, the readiness of the team, and the personalities of the leader and team members. Skill in discrimination is essential for making effective choices. Personal style and theoretical orientation will determine the manner in which the leader uses the understanding and discriminating skills within a team setting. Adherence to theories that are more structured will require teaching or modeling; less structured approaches are better matched with nondirective, self-discovery methods.

The hierarchical nature of the conflict management strategies can be drawn upon to provide a backup or secondary strategy (Kormanski, 1982; Kottler, 1993). If withdrawal is chosen and proves ineffective, the other four choices remain and can be chosen subsequently. If suppression is chosen and fails to work, there are still three additional

TABLE 3.1 *Conflict Management Strategies and Contingencies*

Preferred Strategy	Use When (Advantages)	But Be Aware That (Disadvantages)
Withdrawal	Choosing sides is to be avoided. Others are competent for dealing with the crisis. Critical information is missing. You, as the leader, are powerless. The issue is unimportant.	It cannot be used in a crisis. Legitimate action is no longer possible. Failure is perceived. Access to information ceases. The issue may grow.
Suppression	A relationship is important. A cooling down period is needed. The issue is outside the team.	You, as the leader, appear weak. The issue may intensify.
Consensus	Team commitment is needed. Promoting open communication and trust is desired. New alternatives are needed. Problem solving is needed.	More time is needed. Team goals must be put first. It does not work with rigid, dull people.
Compromise	Resources are limited. A win-win set is desired. Power is equal.	It encourages inflation of needs and wants. It could weaken action. A third party is often needed for negotiation.
Authority	Time is limited (crisis). A deadlock persists. Others are incompetent for dealing with the crisis. An unpopular decision needs to be made. Survival of the organization is critical.	It creates losers. It heightens emotions. It promotes dependency.

Note: Adapted from C. L. Kormanski (1982), "Leadership Strategies for Managing Conflict," *Journal for Specialists in Group Work, 7*(2), 112–118.

alternatives. Authority becomes the ultimate choice of last resort. With its use, the other choices are eliminated.

Consideration of the contingencies presented in Table 3.1 in choosing a conflict management strategy will increase the likelihood of a positive outcome. Choosing a strategy for the wrong reason will eventually compound the conflict situation and make it more difficult to manage. Some examples of the wrong reasons for choosing a strategy follow. Withdrawal could be chosen to avoid disagreements and protect the self from a perceived emotional battle. Suppression could be used to protect or patronize others. Consensus might be selected to buy time and keep others who are competent from making a decision. Compromise might be opted to protect against losses. Authority could be utilized to maintain a high ego involvement for the decision maker. All of these reasons are inappropriate.

In addition to being knowledgeable about conflict and conflict management strategies, the leader must develop the intervention skills of using and combining the strategies for their successful implementation. Successful team leadership encourages conflict and manages it effectively. This combination of dynamic leadership and healthy conflict are prerequisites for a growing, productive group (Kormanski, 1982).

Leadership

4

A leader is a person you will follow to a place you wouldn't go by yourself.

—Joel Barker

Grace, Alex, Ron, and Irma convened for their discussion about leadership at the end of the summer. Grace began by suggesting that effective leadership is contingent upon three things: the abilities of the leader, the characteristics of the group and its individual members, and the situation in which the leader and the group are interacting. "Leading an infantry platoon on an undercover mission," she noted, "is very different from chairing a committee to plan a reception for a visiting artist. Leading a group of ministers can be very different from being in charge of a college fraternity." She added that individual leaders have different values, have been involved in different experiences, and have usually developed a preferred style of leadership that fits their personality and situational role.

Alex noted that leadership styles vary from authoritarian to abdication and that the style is expressed by specific behaviors and the attention given to the three types of needs that exist in any work group. "Task needs," he said, "include commitment, clarification, involvement, achievement, and recognition. Relationship needs include acceptance, belonging, support, pride, and satisfaction. Finally, each group member has individual needs that require attention. These may include needs related to physiological well-being, security, belonging, or esteem. They may also involve higher order needs such as achievement, affiliation, power, or self-actualization."

Ron added that one individual can address all three types of functions: attention to tasks, relationships, and individual needs. There may, instead, be a task leader and a relationship leader. "Sharing the leadership role within functions is also possible," he said, "Each individual varies in the importance and expertise he or she gives to the three functions. Some leaders are more task oriented, whereas others are more relationship oriented. Individual needs sometimes receive attention only when the other two functions are being accomplished adequately."

Irma explained that experience may or may not be the best teacher, but it is certainly not the only one. "In addition to leadership experiences," she said, "there are some specific behavioral skills that can be taught to prospective leaders or further developed by those already in leadership positions." These skills are discussed later in this chapter.

Alex added that awareness and discrimination are prerequisites for effectively utilizing leadership skills. "The leader first must be aware of what is happening with the group and the nature of the situation. Then he or she must use discrimination regarding which skills to use and at what time and level to intervene."

Irma pointed out that understanding and developing the skills for effective leadership can be enhanced by being knowledgeable in three related areas: Theories of psychological development of the individual provide information about people, their growth, and their maturation; group development theories contribute sociological data about how individuals relate to one another interpersonally in small groups; and theories of organizational development offer insight into the dynamics of systems and large-group behavior.

"Leadership," Grace concluded, "is not some mystical quality with which some individuals are gifted and others are not. In some ways, it is a science. Some specific leadership skills and areas of knowledge can be acquired by training. Further, leadership skills can be improved and developed to effective levels of functioning for use within small groups and large organizations. But, as with all skills and knowledge-based concepts, the skills must be practiced and the knowledge must be constantly updated." Ron countered with the fact that leadership in other ways is an art. He quoted Max DePree (1989, p. 3), who wrote, "Leadership is more tribal than scientific, more a weaving of relationships that an amassing of information, and, in that sense, I don't know how to pin it down in every detail."

Each of the four friends had prepared and distributed the results of their research efforts. Ron had examined the area of leadership and knowledge; Alex had addressed leadership and skills; Irma had explored leadership and motivation; and Grace had written about leadership and power. Their summaries follow.

▼ LEADERSHIP AND KNOWLEDGE

For leaders, knowledge acquisition may come from a variety of sources. Many formal training programs are available for leadership development, ranging from seminars of a few hours to multiyear degree programs. Experience is, of course, an invaluable asset, but it takes time to accumulate. In addition, the individual's initiative and risk-taking behavior may expand or limit the amount and variety of experiences he or she has. Self-learning is another method for gaining knowledge. A variety of books, journals, magazines, audiotapes, and videotapes covering leadership topics offer either a specific or a broad focus.

Our national history of leadership in organizations has evolved from a scientific management approach to a social science one (Weisbord, 1987). Along the way, a focus developed regarding the welfare of the employee and eventually a concern for the consumer. Thus, expertise in different forms of leadership was needed. Burns (1978) defined two fundamentally different forms of leadership. Transactional leadership involves the exchange of valued things as its major purpose. Transformational leadership increases awareness and acceptance of higher levels of motivation and morality. Burns's delineation is similar to a comparison Selznick (1957) made between administrative management and institutional leadership. He suggested that leaders who possess a concern for the evolution of the organization make a shift from administrative management to institutional leadership. Kormanski and Mozenter (1987) described the same shift from transactional to transformational leadership within the context of a team development model built upon group development stage theory. Combining group development theory with this shift in leadership philosophy provides a rough guideline of the combination of transactional and transformational leadership needed at each stage of group development. Figure 4.1 illustrates this combination.

DePree (1989) contrasted contractual relationships (management) with covenantal ones (leadership). The contractual relationship forms the basis for transactional leadership. This day-to-day working relationship provides stability and continuity. The work is managed. Someone is minding the store. The covenantal relationship is not found in all organizations, and thus there is a sparsity of transformational leadership. Covenantal relationships involve commitment to organizational ideals and to the people of the organization. This type of relationship is more participative than traditional; it encourages diversity and

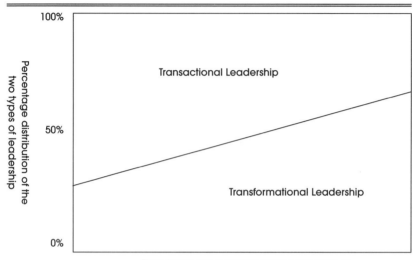

Stages of Development	1. Forming	2. Storming	3. Norming	4. Performing	5. Adjourning
Task Behavior	Orientation	Resistance	Communication	Problem solving	Termination
Relationship Behavior	Dependence	Hostility	Cohesion	Interdependence	Disengagement

Note: Adapted from C. L. Kormanski & A. Mozenter (1987), "A New Model of Team Building: A Technology for Today and Tomorrow," in J. W. Pfeiffer (Ed.), *The 1987 Annual: Developing Human Resources* (pp. 255–268), San Diego, CA: Pfeiffer & Co. Used with permission.

FIGURE 4.1 *Type of Leadership and Group Development Stages*

manageable conflict; it accepts modest failures as learning experiences; and it prizes meaningful work. Both types of relationships and leadership are necessary. The critical factor is knowing how to blend them together based upon the needs of the organization and its people.

▼ LEADERSHIP AND SKILLS

Understanding organizational life involves understanding people and the diversity of their gifts, talents, and skills (DePree, 1989). In any organization there exists a variety of individuals with a variety of skills. Each person has the opportunity to contribute to any task in unique ways. As groups of individuals work together they can accomplish complex tasks in less time than individuals working alone, and through synergistic interaction they can achieve more than individuals working separately. Unfortunately, some gifts and talents go unrecognized and some skills are unused. Effective leadership can offset this situation by providing opportunities for such gifts, talents, and skills to emerge.

One way to organize skills required of leaders is to classify them by function. Leaders are involved in carrying out a number of managerial functions. Skills in this area might include, for example, planning, organizing, and staffing a particular project or ongoing job task. In addition, leaders carry out supervisory functions, which may require the skills of directing, controlling, coordinating, and delegating. According to the models of the sequential group development stages, supervision would involve mostly directing skills in the forming stage, controlling skills in the storming stage, coordinating skills in the norming stage, and delegating skills in the performing stage. The adjourning stage would require a return to increased coordinating skills in order to disband the group or to recycle the group to another task.

However, there are an infinite number of ways to define and categorize skills. Often the same skill has been described by different people in the same manner but given a different name. An attempt has been made here to keep a broad perspective and to focus on those skills that receive primary attention in the literature. Based on the need for leaders to provide both transactional and transformational leadership, identifying the skills that are a part of each type is an important first step.

Bennis and Nanus (1985) suggested that the difference between transactional leadership and transformational leadership is the difference between managing and leading. Kormanski and Mozenter's (1987) model of team building defines specific transactional skills and transformational skills for each of the five stages of group development. Both types of skills are needed for total leadership effectiveness (Barnard, 1938; Burns, 1978; Selznick, 1957). However, as individuals become more experienced and willing to engage in teamwork, they require less direct supervision and more inspiration (Burns, 1978; Ferguson, 1980). During the later stages of group development, members of groups with democratic management styles assume responsibility for many of the transactional leadership outcomes, thus decreasing those task responsibilities for the group leaders and allowing them to give more attention to transformational outcomes.

Although group leaders use the skills of managing and leading throughout the life of the group, a pattern evolves whereby specific skills are used more frequently during specific group stages (Kormanski & Mozenter, 1987). Table 4.1 illustrates this relationship. The transacting skills, defined in texts that focus on the management functions of planning, organizing, motivating, and controlling (Cascio, 1986; Greenlaw & Kohl, 1986; Hellriegal, Slocum & Woodman, 1986; Hersey & Blanchard, 1982; McAfee & Champagne, 1987), can be viewed as forming the following pattern. Getting-acquainted, goal-setting, and organizing skills are dominant during stage 1. In stage 2, the skills of active listening, assertiveness, and conflict management come to the fore. Communication, feedback, and affirmation skills are most needed in stage 3, and decision-making, problem-solving, and rewarding skills are called upon in stage 4. Finally, stage 5 involves evaluating and reviewing.

The transformational skills are currently receiving increased attention, although Barnard (1938) and Selznick (1957) were early advocates. Interest heightened in the 1980s when it became apparent that the increased rapidity of change in organizations required visionary leadership (Burns, 1978; Ferguson, 1980; Kanter, 1983; Kormanski & Mozenter, 1987; Peters & Waterman, 1982). Transformational skills provide an additional dimension to the management function of

TABLE 4.1 *Leadership Skills*

Group Development Stage	Task and Relationship Behaviors	Skills by Function	Transactional Skills (Management)	Transformational Skills (Leadership)
1. Forming	Orientation and dependence	Directing	Getting acquainted Goal setting Organizing	Values clarification Visioning Communication through myth and metaphor
2. Storming	Resistance and hostility	Controlling	Active listening Assertiveness Conflict management	Flexibility Creativity Kaleidoscopic thinking
3. Norming	Communication and cohesion	Coordinating	Communicating Feedback Affirmation	Playfulness and humor Entrepreneurship Networking
4. Performing	Problem solving and interdependence	Delegating	Decision making Problem solving Rewarding	Multicultural awareness Mentoring Futuring
5. Adjourning	Termination and disengagement	Coordinating	Evaluating Reviewing	Celebrating Bringing closure

Note: Adapted from C. L. Kormanski & A. Mozenter, (1987), "A New Model of Team Building: A Technology for Today and Tomorrow," in J. W. Pfeiffer (Ed.), *The 1987 Annual: Developing Human Resources* (pp. 255–268), San Diego, CA: Pfeiffer & Co. Used with permission.

leaders. Selznick (1957) viewed the function of transformational leadership as being an educational process with the role of leadership focusing on building the institution's human and technological resources in a manner that promotes and protects the values and mission of the organization.

The transformational skills have been defined in the writings of Barnard (1938), Block (1987), Burns (1978), Ferguson (1980), Kanter (1983), Peters and Waterman (1982), Selznick (1957), and Senge (1990) and have been paired with stages of group development by Kormanski and Mozenter (1987). During the forming stage, the skills of values clarification (understanding the importance of one's values), visioning (linking mission and purpose with the future), and communicating through myth and metaphor (using stories and anecdotes to describe philosophy and define culture) are helpful. During the storming stage, the skills of flexibility (developing openness and versatility), creativity (promoting new ideas and encouraging experimentation), and kaleidoscopic thinking (discovering new ways of viewing old problems) are often called upon. The skills of playfulness and humor (integrating the spirit of fun into work), entrepreneurship (supporting independence and competitiveness), and networking (building coalitions of support) are often used during the norming stage, and the skills of multicultural awareness (understanding cultural differences), mentoring (sharing one's wisdom and experiences), and futuring (forecasting outcomes through trend analysis) contribute to the success of the performing stage. Finally, the adjourning stage profits from the skills of celebrating (using ceremony to acknowledge accomplishment) and closure (ending a particular task or group). Figure 4.2 summarizes the transformational skills.

▼ LEADERSHIP AND MOTIVATION

One cannot motivate someone else, although this request is frequently made of leadership. Motivation comes from within. Since leaders are external to followers, they influence through the use of power. The role of leadership in relation to motivation is to give followers the opportunity to get what they want or need. Thus, understanding the needs of individuals and groups becomes a prerequisite to providing opportunities that can aid individuals in their personal and professional development.

The work of Abraham Maslow (1954, 1971) offers a comprehensive understanding of motivation and its influence on personality.

Values Clarification: Understanding the importance of one's values.

Visioning: Linking mission and purpose with the future.

Communicating Through Myth and Metaphor: Using stories and anecdotes to describe philosophy and define culture.

Flexibility: Developing openness and versatility.

Creativity: Promoting new ideas and encouraging experimentation.

Kaleidoscopic Thinking: Discovering new ways of viewing old problems.

Playfulness and Humor: Integrating the spirit of fun into the workplace.

Entrepeneurship: Supporting independence and competitiveness.

Networking: Building coalitions of support.

Multicultural Awareness: Understanding cultural differences.

Mentoring: Sharing one's wisdom and experiences.

Futuring: Forecasting outcomes through trend analysis.

Celebrating: Using ceremony to acknowledge accomplishment.

Bringing Closure: Ending a particular task or group.

Note: Adapted from C. L. Kormanski & A. Mozenter (1987), "A New Model of Team Building: A Technology for Today and Tomorrow," in J. W. Pfeiffer (Ed.), *The 1987 Annual: Developing Human Resources* (pp. 255–268), San Diego, CA: Pfeiffer & Co. Used with permission.

FIGURE 4.2 *Transformational Skills*

Maslow created a hierarchy of need levels and suggested that when a need is unfulfilled, the lower on the hierarchy the need is located, the more powerful will be its influence on the personality. To some extent, all needs are somewhat unfulfilled and somewhat fulfilled. As the gap widens and the need becomes more unfulfilled, the need demands more attention, and this demand is even further increased if the need is low on the hierarchy. Needs can be compared to a city skyline. As one moves about a city, one's view of the skyline changes; similarly, the nature of our needs changes continually.

Physiological needs are at the bottom of Maslow's hierarchy and involve food, shelter, clothing, and related survival needs. In addition, health-related issues, including occupational stress, are a part of this need level. Salary and other income are a major resource for fulfilling these needs. The more unjust the salary for a particular job, the more motivated the individual will be to seek another job and the more dissatisfied the individual will be with the current situation. Frequent discussion among employees about cost-of-living issues reflects the strength of physiological needs.

As physiological needs become fulfilled, safety and security needs require increased attention. In the organization these needs become apparent in expressions of concern for job security, health and retirement benefits, and safety features. Security needs are also evidenced by a concern for information about the future. Knowing what is going on and what to expect in their jobs allows people to use goal setting to structure their work life and gain more control over their immediate environment. The absence of this information creates uncertainty and increasing anxiety, which can interfere with the workday, and encourages the collection of information from sources that may be unreliable. But then, questionable information is perceived as being more helpful than no information at all.

The next level in the hierarchy consists of needs focused on belonging. Social interaction and inclusion issues are important. Such needs are more apparent in organizations today than in the past, as the workplace is fast becoming one of the major socializing agencies in our culture. In this age of changing family structures, increased mobility, and urban/suburban environments, the workplace provides a stable setting that is similar to the family and small-town community of past eras. Today's emphasis on corporate cultures and values gives credence to this process, which is enhanced by company celebrations, recreational groups, welfare projects, community outreach efforts, and other social involvement activities occurring as a part of organizational life.

Needs of esteem are next on the hierarchy. Being recognized and honored becomes important as lower needs are fulfilled. In the organization, peer recognition, approval from authority figures, and self-esteem issues surface. Developing appropriate recognition is a constant challenge for those in supervisory positions. Blanchard and Johnson's (1982) advice in *The One Minute Manager* is for supervisors to catch people doing something right and then praise them. Self-esteem is continually identified as an area requiring improvement in our educational system, but it is often neglected in the workplace.

At the top of the hierarchy are self-actualization needs and what Maslow called the higher needs. Self-actualization is an ongoing process of experiencing life fully. It involves making growth choices, assessing oneself honestly, recognizing peak experiences, and developing one's potential. An effort is made to understand what one values and create a consistency among one's values, attitudes, and behaviors. In essence, self-actualized people live their beliefs. They are their values.

In Maslow's theory, higher needs are the pathways to self-actualization and represent the "characteristics of being" or the "values of being." Maslow identified 14 value groups, including truth, goodness, beauty, justice, simplicity, playfulness, and self-sufficiency. Another view of higher needs was offered by David McClelland (1961), who suggested that the needs of achievement, affiliation, and power are important sources of motivation. In the organization, individuals with high achievement needs set challenging but realistic goals, are modest risk takers, and desire performance feedback. Those with high affiliation needs are more concerned with promoting harmonious relationships, developing mutual trust and respect, and giving attention to the human side of the organization. People with high power needs seek out conflict, prefer a political climate, and use persuasive skills to advance within the organization.

Herzberg (1966) devised a motivational theory that divided Maslow's hierarchical concepts into hygiene factors and motivators. In the organization, hygiene factors include a just salary, benefits, job security, safety, health, satisfactory supervisory behavior, and positive work relationships. Motivators are the needs located on the top part of Maslow's hierarchy. They include challenging work, decision-making opportunities, self-esteem, responsibility, career advancement, and participative involvement. Herzberg suggested that hygiene factors are not motivational but create dissatisfaction when absent.

Too often, jobs have excellent salaries and security but lack motivational elements or have exceptional motivational opportunities but have low salaries and marginal security. Weisbord (1987) noted that the early history of management-labor relations was characterized by management mistaking hygiene factors for motivators. Once individuals became experienced at most of their assigned tasks and fulfilled many of their basic needs, they were ready for motivators such as those Herzberg identified. However, the adversarial relationship between management and labor focused almost entirely on disagreements over hygiene needs.

Group development experiences offer another, less complex, illustration of motivation. As a group moves through the forming and storming stages and the members gain an understanding of the difficulty and complexity of the tasks of the group, there is a shift from a willingness to an unwillingness to participate. This results in a decrease in motivation of group members. By the norming stage, motivators are needed to sustain the growth of the group and combat the members' unwillingness and/or unconfidence. If these motivators are absent, the development of the group slows and the possibility for apathy or chaos to occur increases dramatically.

Specific types of needs are apparent at each stage of group development as a result of the combination of the willingness/unwillingness and the experience/inexperience of the group members. As the group develops, the members, as a unit, move upward on the Maslow hierarchy (Kormanski, 1985). Individuals may continue to experience a variety of needs, but the group and most of its members will demonstrate needs consistent with the group development stage. Thus, physiological and safety/security needs will predominate during the forming stage when everyone is new to the task (and possibly to the group) and many are feeling a lot of uncertainty. During the storming stage, conflict is fueled by the strong need to belong. During the norming stage, in which the group membership is often characterized as being unwilling or unconfident but experienced, many individuals wrestle with high esteem needs. Behavior during the performing stage reflects Maslow's higher needs, McClelland's needs of achievement, affiliation, and power, as well as many of Herzberg's motivators (Hersey & Blanchard, 1982). With the advent of the adjourning stage comes a retreat to the needs of esteem and recognition seen in the norming stage (Kormanski, 1985). Table 4.2 demonstrates this relationship between group

TABLE 4.2 *Group Development Stages and Motivational Levels*

Group Development Stage	Individual Needs	Willingness Description*	Experience Description*
1. Forming	Physiological and safety/security	Eager and willing	Inexperienced
2. Storming	Belonging and social	Unwilling or unconfident	Inexperienced
3. Norming	Esteem and recognition	Unwilling or unconfident	Experienced
4. Performing	Higher needs and self-actualization	Eager and willing	Experienced
5. Adjourning	Esteem and recognition	Unwilling or unconfident	Experienced

*Willingness and experience levels are assessed in relation to a specific task of the group.

Note: Adapted from C. L. Kormanski (1985), "A Situational Leadership™ Approach to Groups Using the Tuckman Model of Group Development," in L. D. Goodstein & J. W. Pfeiffer (Eds.), *The 1985 Annual: Developing Human Resources* (pp. 217–225), San Diego, CA: Pfeiffer & Co. Used with permission.

development stages and motivational levels, identifying the individual needs and willingness and experience levels at each stage.

The following scenario provides a practical illustration of how motivational theories can be drawn upon to understand team needs and direct leaders to appropriate intervention strategies based upon those needs. Training sessions for frontline supervisors were being conducted in an organization that had decided to reduce salaries in order to survive in a very competitive marketplace. At the start of the first weekly training session, all of the supervisors noted that they had agreed to accept a 10% wage reduction in order to keep their jobs and to keep the plant from closing. The session was appropriately titled "Power and Motivation."

The strategy that had been developed by top management for the labor force, which had also accepted a pay reduction, was to provide increased opportunities for motivator-type needs to be fulfilled. The supervisors had a "gut" feeling that this strategy would not work. Following an examination of the motivational theories of Maslow and Herzberg, they became convinced that different strategies were needed. In essence, top management was proposing to replace unfulfilled lower needs with opportunities to fulfill higher needs, a tradeoff that is not consistent with Maslow's hierarchy.

So, rather than focusing on motivator-type needs, the supervisors spent much of the session developing strategies for fulfilling security and belonging needs (much lower on the hierarchy) that they could implement quickly. Examining nonmaterialistic rewards was a key focus. The supervisors moved the topic of improving skill in relationship behavior forward from later in the training program, and they decided to make the goal of the next session determining ways to use various power bases in combination with motivation.

The complexity of the human personality frequently results in behavior that has more than one source of influence. Motivation and power more often than not occur in some combination. The following example illustrates this point. A high school student practiced all summer for a fall tennis tournament. She was a competitive individual with a strong desire to win. Her efforts paid off; she was victorious in the tournament. As she celebrated her success, she became aware that in addition to being influenced by a strong achievement motivation, she was also influenced by the $1,000 college scholarship award offered by the local tennis club and the attractive trophy, which were examples of reward power.

▼ LEADERSHIP AND POWER

As modern organizations evolve, there is a movement from the practice of management through power to a process of leadership through persuasion (DePree, 1989). According to Rosebeth Moss Kanter (1983), "The degree to which the opportunity to use power effectively [that is, persuasively] is granted to or withheld from individuals is one operative difference between companies which stagnate and those which innovate" (p. 18). The current trends of employee involvement and employee empowerment are relevant examples of this change. The movement from transactional leadership to transformational leadership follows the same course, with transactional leadership relying on management through power and transformational leadership relying on persuasion.

Machiavelli (1952) described two major types of power: position power and personal power. Position power is dominant in any influential relationship based on fear, and personal power is dominant in any such relationship based on love. DePree's leadership through persuasion resembles Machiavelli's personal power, and his management through power reflects Machiavelli's position power.

Position power bases having the ability and resources to influence using *rewards* and *coercive means* (Cummings, 1981; French & Raven, 1959); having *connective power,* which involves having the backing and support of other powerful individuals (Cummings, 1981; Hersey et al., 1979) including one's supervisor; and having *legitimate power,* which is directly related to the official position of the individual in the organization (Cummings, 1981; French & Raven, 1959). This position is often defined formally by rules, by regulations, and, when a union is involved, by a contract.

Personal power bases include *expert power,* which involves one's expertise, skill, and knowledge (Cummings, 1981; French & Raven, 1959); *referent power,* which involves one's personal traits, such as likability, trustworthiness, sincerity, and respect (Cummings, 1981; French & Raven, 1959); and *informational power,* which pertains to what a person knows about the organization and his or her access to informational sources (Hersey et al., 1979; Raven & Kruglanski, 1975).

These seven power bases are all essential to the leadership process. Typical examples of the use of power in an organization are praise by a manager (reward power), ridicule by a colleague (coercive power), support from a supervisor (connective power), use of a grievance procedure (legitimate power), loyalty from employees (referent power), publication of a company newsletter (informational power), and task force recommendations (expert power). However, the position power bases are most useful when the leadership is more transactional, and the personal power bases are most useful when the leadership is more transformational. Therefore, individuals in the early stages of group development respond more to position power, while those in the later stages are more influenced by personal power. In fact, switching the power bases can have an effect similar to that of mismatching jumper cables on an automobile battery. Using position power, particularly coercive power, on experienced group members can be very explosive, and personal power used on inexperienced group members often has no effect (Kormanski, 1988). One point of note about coercive power: It can be very emotional and unpredictable, and it rarely contributes to positive group development. Therefore, it should be used as sparingly as possible and only as a last resort when the survival of the organization or other group is at stake.

Cohen and Smith (1976) leant support to the viewpoint that different types of power are more effective at different stages of group development through their description of group member evolution from initial dependence on the position of the leader to increased feelings of personal competence and inner-directed power by the termination stage. The 10 stages in their group development model are related to Tuckman's generic five-stage model. Thus, group members move from dependence (forming) to counterdependence (storming) to independence (norming) to interdependence (performing) and back to independence (adjourning) when the group concludes. This pattern also follows the Bennis and Shepard (1956) model of group development noted earlier. Table 4.3 illustrates the relationship between group development and power.

▼ DISCUSSION OF LEADERSHIP

Alex, Grace, Irma, and Ron congratulated one another for their comprehensive investigation of the components of leadership. Then Alex asserted that managing change is an important desired outcome of

TABLE 4.3 *Group Development and Power*

Group Development Stage Tuckman & Jensen (1977)	Group Leader Power Base Machiavelli (1952)	Group Member Power State Bennis & Shepard (1956)
1. Forming	Position	Dependence
2. Storming	Position	Counterdependence
3. Norming	Personal	Independence
4. Performing	Personal	Interdependence
5. Adjourning	Personal	Independence

leadership and that leadership influences change. He noted that knowledge and understanding represent only one part of the overall dynamics of leadership, and a small part at that. "Many individuals," he said, "understand and know what needs to be done but do not possess the skill or ability to deliver an effective intervention. Recognizing that a team member needs assistance in clarifying a specific work role is one thing; delivering a high task/high relationship leader intervention that manages this conflict is another. Using your past experience to empathize with a coworker over a particularly frustrating project that you feel she is capable of solving given time and providing her with encouragement without patronizing while she is working on the project require different types of competencies. The former involves knowledge and understanding, while the latter involves skill and ability. Both are a part of effective leadership."

Grace contributed the insight that if leadership is influence, then the potential to influence is power. "Understanding and knowing what to do and having the skill to do it are useless to a leader," she said, "if no one chooses to be influenced by and to follow him or her. There are two basic reasons why someone might choose to follow. One is externally based and involves another's use of personal or position power.

The other is internally based and is related to motivation. When an individual acts because of being influenced by someone or something outside the self, power is being used. When an individual acts to fulfill an inner need, desire, or want, the influential source is motivation."

Irma, who had recently served as an officer in the state counseling association as well as chairing its recent conference, commented that their leadership discussion validated many of her experiences in these roles. She noted five insights she derived from holding these positions: (1) Understand how the system works, since many problems involve the system and change interventions need to begin there. (2) View conflict as a friend. Healthy conflict is a prerequisite to growth and development. Examine chaos theory, and use a variety of the conflict management techniques noted in Chapter 3. (3) See competence and experience as prerequisites to empowerment. Use early team life to build and develop team members' abilities, then empower the team members to solve problems. (4) Involve everyone in the change process by encouraging task achievement and supporting meaningful relationships. (5) Celebrate often; tell stories, retell myths, create visions for the future, and have fun.

Ron noted that the five leader functions Irma mentioned occurred sequentially during the five stages of group development. He then mentioned five trends that he felt described the progression of teams and their leaders throughout the life of the group. Whereas Irma's insights were more stage specific, the trends Ron mentioned were broad and more comprehensive. He suggested the following: (1) Supervision demands movement from a directive style to a democratic one. (2) Team members satisfy their basic needs and then increase their desire to fulfill higher ones. (3) Opportunities decrease for transactional leadership and increase for transformational leadership. (4) Power bases for influence shift from positional to personal. (5) Groups frequently become teams.

The leadership discussion stimulated another round of possible topics for investigation, and each member was eager to continue exploring the dynamics of leadership. Grace wanted to put into writing the leadership model that was developing from their discussions; Alex wanted to investigate how the model might be applied in organizations;

Irma chose to research visionary leadership; and Ron wanted to share with the others the details of a recent humorous incident. The team's summaries follow.

▼ A LEADERSHIP MODEL

The leadership model presented in Figure 4.3 delineates the four key components of leadership: knowledge, skills, power, and motivation. The desired outcome, or goal, is behavioral change, and the process toward change is identified as a series of stages of group development (forming, storming, norming, performing, and adjourning). The presence of conflict symbolizes that leadership and conflict are inseparable (Burns, 1978). The more conflict in a group or organization, the more the need for leadership. Leadership, then, is about influencing change within a conflicted environment by utilizing knowledge, skills, power, and motivation to enable individuals and teams to develop the capacity to achieve their goals and inspire others. In its purest sense, effective leadership develops additional effective leaders.

A.   Desired Outcome: Behavioral change

B.   Leadership Components: Knowledge
Skills
Power
Motivation

C.   Major Challenge: Managing conflict

D.   Group/Team Process: Forming
Storming
Norming
Performing
Adjourning

FIGURE 4.3 *A Leadership Model*

▼ APPLYING THE MODEL

Organizations and their component groups, in their quest to be more productive, might consider using the leadership model presented in this chapter as a focal point. Indeed, the literature has been encouraging this type of focus for the past decade. Kanter (1983) noted that three sets of skills are required to provide effective leadership in settings that stress participative teams: Power skills are needed to influence others to invest information, support, and resources in new initiatives; teamwork skills are needed to manage groups and utilize employee participation; and an understanding of the dynamics of organizational change is required. McAfee and Champagne (1987) suggested the following three ways to increase production: improving the skills and abilities of the group members, developing team functioning, and improving the motivational level of the group members by providing opportunities for them to fulfill their needs. DePree (1989) noted that controlling change, managing conflicts, and enabling others to reach their potential were all part of the art of leadership. Similar ideas for managing change and providing the transformational leadership to inspire excellence have been provided by Ferguson (1980), Bennis and Nanus (1985), and Peters and Waterman (1982).

Clover (1990) described attention to transformational leadership as a movement away from the rational models of leadership and toward more emotional ones. Hersey and Blanchard's (1982) situational model, Fiedler's (1967) contingency model, House's (1971) path-goal theory, Vroom and Yetton's (1973) decision-making model, and Blake and Mouton's (1964) managerial grid have provided a rational approach to leadership and are usually implemented with the use of transactional skills. The transformational skills, which are much more emotional in nature, are components of the more recent leadership concepts of Burns (1978), Bass (1985), Bennis and Nanus (1985), and Kouzes and Posner (1987). Blanchard's (1996) Situational Leadership II model is an example of a revision of an earlier model to make it more transformational.

Both approaches—transactional and transformational—are needed. It is the balance that is essential. As Jung (1971) noted in his studies of personality, some people have a preference for thinking (rational approach) and others have a preference for feeling (emotional approach) when making decisions. A working model of leadership must be both transactional and transformational. The rational must be balanced with the emotional. More transactional leadership is needed in the early stages of group life when individuals are inexperienced in relation to the task. Transformational leadership is used more toward the later stages of group life when individuals are more task experienced. The use of only one approach upsets the balance. Fortunately, the rational models of leadership have the potential to be expanded to include the transformational components now being developed.

▼ VISIONARY LEADERSHIP

In 1957, Selznick stressed the importance of values, myths, and creativity for school administrators. He cited integrity as a primary value for leaders and monitoring the environment for threats, seeking opportunities for change, and building a team to ensure survival of the organization as their primary tasks. Twenty-five years later, Peters and Waterman (1982) stated that the most important factor in organizational survival is adherence to one's values and beliefs. They described values as being almost always qualitative and inspiring people throughout the organization. In 1996, Bennis and Mische, like others before them, advocated visioning as a process for influencing change. They encouraged leaders to be achievement motivated; to create a sense of energy, passion, and commitment; and to be bold and strive for quantum rather than the incremental change.

Block (1987) integrated empowerment into the visioning process by encouraging leaders to choose greatness over maintenance; courage over caution, and autonomy over dependence. He saw the major visioning tasks of leaders as developing, communicating, and applying their vision in a manner that promotes sharing and support. In a more recent book, Block (1993) suggested stewardship as an alternative to leadership. He advocated some challenging systems changes including doing more with less, learning to pay attention to customers, and creating employees who are committed and passionate.

Senge (1990) identified shared vision as one of his five disciplines of learning organizations. A shared vision provides both a focus and the energy to pursue that focus for an extended time. New ways of thinking and acting are encouraged. Risk taking and experimenting are supported. Finally, a shared vision links the day-to-day problems to the future of the organization.

Visionary leadership provides the setting in which one can live one's values. It ties beliefs to performance. Visionary leaders are champions of causes, believe in themselves, learn from others, embrace diversity, extend boundaries, promote team development, and celebrate team successes.

▼ THE STEPHANIE SYNDROME

Rather than submitting a research summary, Ron described verbally an insight that came to him after watching a rerun on television. He discussed an early episode of "The Bob Newhart Show" involving the maid, Stephanie, breaking up with her boyfriend. After a few days had passed, Stephanie became painfully aware that breaking up was not a smart decision to have made. Her boyfriend had been her social life. He had chauffeured her around town, taken her shopping, provided evenings out for dinner, movies, and other leisure events. Without him, she had no social life, for she had depended on him to respond to all of her specific requests, make appropriate arrangements, provide funding, and cater to her every whim.

Recognizing the error of her ways, she quickly reacted to remedy the situation. Encountering her boyfriend in the lobby of the country inn where she was employed, she emphatically stated, "We have to get back together immediately! What's the least I can do to get back together with you? And I mean the *very least!*"

This episode provided a few chuckles for Ron at the time, but it took on added significance the following week when fall semester classes began at the campus where Ron was teaching. During a discussion of wants and expectations of course content and process, he heard students saying "We want A's and B's. What's the least we can do to get these? And we mean the *very least!*" They continued by emphasizing that they did not want exams, quizzes, term papers, attendance require-ments, evaluations of class discussions, or group projects. They just wanted good grades for minimum effort.

As the months progressed, Ron found what he called "Stephanie syndromes" all over the place. He listened to employees in a variety of work environments identifying their daily goals with words like, "I just want to get through the day. I don't want any hassles; I don't want coworkers bothering me; I don't want to have to engage in any extended concentration or effort. So, what's the least I can do today? And I mean the *very least*?"

As Ron thought more about this attitudinal syndrome, he began to feel apprehensive. What if the person filling his medical prescription had shown up for work with the Stephanie syndrome? What if the syn-drome were contagious and had spread to the police force, the school-teachers, the auto mechanics, and the nuclear engineers? How widespread was the problem?

Upon doing a little research, Ron found an interesting study con-ducted by William James (Hersey & Blanchard, 1982). James was investigating motivation in the workplace. He found that hourly employees, when highly motivated, could work at 80–90% of their potential. However, to avoid being fired and to maintain their jobs, they could get by with 30% effort. Thirty percent of output in the workplace, then, is directly related to power, while 50–60% is directly related to motivation. The 20–30% difference represents the effect of the Stephanie syndrome in action.

This insight became more concrete for Ron one Friday morning as he was driving to his university. The week had been filled with con-flict, much of which was still unresolved, and Ron was frustrated over his inability to influence a number of critical events. He heard himself say aloud, "What's the least I can do to get through the day and into my weekend, when I can go home to my family for a few days of peace and quiet?" He had caught the Stephanie syndrome. He now realized that everyone gets it and no one is immune. Ron began call-ing the syndrome the common cold of motivation. He wrote the fol-lowing paragraphs to address this illness and suggest some possible remedies.

All of us catch the common cold of motivation at some time in our lives. For some, the illness is short and simple; for others, it dominates our lifestyle for long periods of time. It encourages apathy and withdrawal from relationships. It has the potential to become depression.

Mentally healthy people have discovered a variety of interventions that alleviate the symptoms until it is caught again. These interventions involve people, places, and activities that renew and reenergize both the body and the spirit. Each of us would do well to develop a list of items for each of these three categories for future use with our clients, our friends, and ourselves.

Ron then told the team how a neighbor of his, who held a middle management position, had recently talked to him about an employee she supervises. She described the employee as having a low level of motivation. She wanted this employee to volunteer for an innovative cross-training program their company was offering. "But I do my current job so well, and I am very comfortable," the employee explained. "There is no one to replace me, and I don't think I have the time and energy needed for this project. I am also somewhat hesitant to work with the people from the marketing department who have volunteered. They appear so assertive." Each strategy the neighbor attempted was countered by more resistance. "I just want to do my job and not get overly involved in company politics and these new fads," the employee would say.

Ron listened attentively to his neighbor and then shared his Stephanie syndrome story. He encouraged his neighbor to focus on this employee's strong security and belonging needs and then weave the challenge of getting the employee to volunteer for the program into an opportunity to fulfill those needs. After some thoughtful dialogue, she devised a plan that involved pairing her reluctant employee with a colleague whom she admired and with whom she had recently worked on a successful project team. The pair would be asked to identify prospective participants for the program after experiencing it themselves. Over time, the neighbor envisioned continuing this process and creating a team of individuals cross-trained in a variety of company functions.

As the neighbor outlined a sequence for implementing this strategy, she had a new insight. "My supervisor must be having a similar experience with me," she noted. "Just last month he suggested that I would be an excellent representative from our unit for a reengineering team that is to be formed soon, but I talked him into selecting someone else because I really prefer the safe structure of organizing the cross-functional training effort, which fits with tasks I have completed in the past."

Ron summarized by stating that leaders must frequently assess team member needs and seek out opportunities for them which can fulfill those needs. Team members who have become too comfortable with their tasks may need to be stimulated and challenged in order to continue their professional (and in many cases, personal) growth. Some individuals may need direction. Some may need support. Many will need both direction and support. A few will only need to be empowered.

▼ CONCLUDING DISCUSSION

As the team completed their initial review of leadership, all were pleased with what they had accomplished. However, the ensuing discussion only raised more questions about leadership. Irma wanted to understand leadership development and how to assess the readiness level of individuals and groups to participate in tasks. Alex was convinced that different situations required differing types of leadership behaviors. Grace was interested in exploring further the relationship between power and leadership. Ron saw leadership applications in organizations as an important topic to research.

All realized that further discussion of applications and relevant experiences would aid them in integrating the various components of leadership, and they looked forward to having the opportunity to continue to grow professionally as a team and as individuals. Leadership style seemed an appropriate topic for their next writing assignments, as all had raised questions and research ideas that fell into this category.

Leadership Style

When actions are performed with unnecessary speech, the people say we did it ourselves.

—Lao Tsu

When Irma, Alex, Grace, and Ron next came together, it was early fall and a new school year had started. Their current writings were more extensive and more probing than earlier efforts. Irma had researched leadership development and readiness. Alex had examined situational leadership. Grace had explored leadership style and power. Ron had addressed the challenge of effective leadership in task group applications. Their writings follow.

▼ LEADERSHIP DEVELOPMENT

Weisbord (1987) provided a comprehensive review of the four major approaches to modern management. He began in 1900 with Frederick Taylor's scientific management approach, which emphasized efficient task accomplishment. He next focused on Kurt Lewin and the human relations approach, which added relationship to the task concern. Then he discussed the behavioral science approach of Douglas McGregor, which encouraged the development of trust in workers along with continued emphasis on both task and relationship behavior. Finally, he described the sociotechnical-systems approach of Fred Emery and Eric Trist, which combined elements of the previous three approaches and encouraged management to create organizational structures that accommodate human needs, technological concerns, and environmental pressures.

The period between World War I and World War II spawned the beginning of interest in leadership development. With U.S. involvement in World War II imminent, providing for the identification of potential military leaders became crucial; after the war, the leadership focus was on integrating veterans back into society. Hollander and Offerman (1990) summarized a variety of approaches to studying leadership during the past 50 years. Emphasis was initially on the discovery of inborn traits critical to leadership. Attention to situational variables followed, as different tasks and interpersonal contexts suggested different styles. Leader attributes then came back into focus with emphasis being given to personality characteristics, motivation, and competence and how these are perceived by followers. As each approach built on its predecessor, more complex models followed. The contingency and transactional approaches provide an example. Contingency models considered leader qualities and situational demands as being interactive, while the transactional models emphasized the social exchange between leaders and followers. Most recently, concern has been given to transformational models.

Both transactional and transformational leadership are needed. The former ties the present to the past and keeps the organization operational; the latter ties the present to the future and creates new methods and directions. As noted in Chapter 4, different skills are used with each type of leadership, and additional knowledge concerning organizational change is required for transformational leadership. The pattern of group development remains the same, however, as do the motivational levels and the power bases for each stage.

▼ TASK READINESS

The dynamic element that brings together the leader and the follower is style. Leadership style involves the combining of task behaviors and relationship behaviors to meet the needs of followers with regard to a specific task. Leadership is inseparable from follower needs and goals (Burns, 1978), and leadership style is always task relevant (Hersey & Blanchard, 1982). Effective leaders look at the readiness of the team and each team member to do each task.

Since their purposes are related, both leader and follower must recognize the other as a person. Undergirding this interactive relationship are the core conditions of unconditional positive regard, congruence or genuineness, and empathic understanding (Rogers, 1961). These conditions are both skills and attitudes about human nature. They are prerequisites to healthy interpersonal relationships as well as to productive work relationships and helping relationships.

Unconditional positive regard or respect involves acceptance and inclusion of the other person. It has become particularly critical with increases in diversity in the workplace. At the job, one does not have to approve of another person's behavior, agree with that person's attitudes, or accept that person's values. But, one does need to treat the other individual as a person of worth.

The second condition, congruence or genuineness, consists of being the person one truly is. Does what we experience on the inside become apparent through our communication with the other person? Too often, we present ourselves as more than what we are through exaggeration, rationalization, and deceptions, or we present ourselves as less than what we are by seeking pity, sympathy, and dependency. Sometimes we act like optimists, and at other times we are pessimists. Becoming self-actualized, as noted in Chapter 4, is frequently a goal of human development, and this process involves living one's values.

Empathic understanding is the final core condition. Empathy is understanding another person at a feeling level. The Native American called it walking a mile in another's moccasins. The skill of empathy involves a sensitivity to the inner world of another person. This skill is enhanced by shared experiences. Thus, we have more accurate empathy for those with whom we have close relationships, and we must work harder to be empathic toward those who are different from us in terms of gender, religion, culture, and geographic setting. More active listening is required as diversity increases, whereas with very close relationships feelings are frequently understood through nonverbal communication alone. These core conditions are used by those in leadership positions to understand the needs of those they supervise.

Being aware of the group development stage and the motivational level of the group members is a helpful focus from a broad perceptive, but a more specific focus for understanding needs is to assess the group or individual's ability and willingness to accomplish a given task. Hersey and Blanchard (1982) called this concept the task maturity level and described it as consisting of a job maturity function and a psychological maturity function. Job maturity assessed one's responsibility to do the task and past experience and/or training regarding the task. It also considered general problem-solving ability, meeting deadlines, knowledge of the task, follow through, and understanding of the task. Psychological maturity assessed willingness to be responsible and achievement motivation regarding the task. It also considered commitment, persistence, independence, initiative, and positive attitude.

Hersey and Blanchard (1989) added task maturity level to their task and relationship behavior matrix as a third dimension to form their Situational Leadership model. They assessed task maturity, as described previously, based on the two functions of ability to do the task and willingness to do the task. This resulted in four task maturity levels, as shown in Figure 5.1. Level one (M1) was characterized by the individual or group being unable or inexperienced and unwilling or unconfident. Level two (M2) signified a change from unwilling to willing, and level three (M3) signified a change from unable to able. Level four (M4) was characterized by the individual or group being able and willing.

Hersey and Blanchard (1996) continued to develop their original theory, but from two differing viewpoints of the concept of task maturity

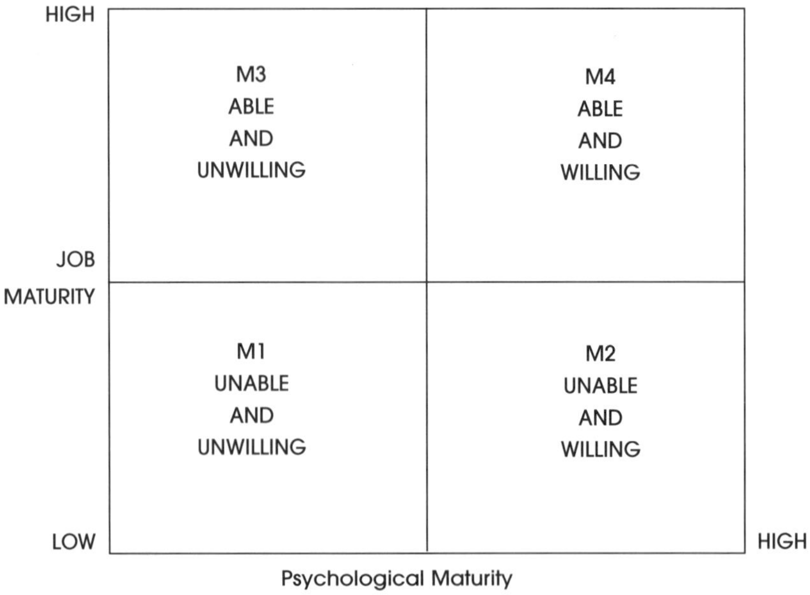

Note: Adapted from P. Hersey & K. H. Blanchard (1982), *Management of Organizational Behavior: Utilizing Human Resources* (4th ed., pp. 150–155), Englewood Cliffs, NJ: Prentice-Hall.

FIGURE 5.1 *Hersey and Blanchard's Task Maturity Levels*

level. Hersey (1984) maintained their initial concept of task maturity but changed the name to readiness, because the task maturity label often got confused with the concept of developmental maturity. Blanchard also renamed task maturity, calling it developmental (D) level (Blanchard, Zigarmi, & Zigarmi, 1985). However, he reversed their original descriptions of level one (M1) and level two (M2). With his terminology, the first level (D1) is defined as being willing and unable and the second level (D2) is defined as being unwilling and unable. Blanchard used the work of Lacoursiere (1980) on group development stages to support this change.

The controversial question revolves around how one should describe an inexperienced group facing a new task in a typical work setting. Are the members willing or unwilling? When an inexperienced employee tackles a new job, is she willing or unwilling? Upon a reexamination of the group development dynamics of the storming stage, solicitation of evaluative comments from frontline managers, and discussions with and reading of recent writers, Blanchard's definitions appear more realistic. This reversal is more consistent with group development theory, as group members are more dependent (willing) and in need of orientation (inexperienced) during the forming stage and more unwilling (hostile) and inexperienced (resistant) during the storming stage (Carew, Parisi-Carew, & Blanchard, 1990). Table 5.1 presents the task maturity revision using Blanchard's developmental levels.

As noted previously, the adjourning stage creates a minor crisis for the group that changes the willingness or confidence back to unwillingness or unconfidence (Kormanski, 1985). As a result, the adjourning stage description of group members is similar to that for the norming stage. (This will be noted again when leadership styles are discussed.) The relationship between the developmental level of followers, the task and relationship behavior of leaders, and the stages of group development forms the basis for Blanchard's Situational Leadership II model (Blanchard et al., 1985).

▼ SITUATIONAL LEADERSHIP

The Situational Leadership model provides an excellent vehicle for discussing leadership styles (Blanchard et al. 1985; Hersey, 1984; Hersey

TABLE 5.1 *Task Maturity Revision*

Developmental Level	Revised Definition	Group Development Stage
D1	Low readiness Eager, enthusiastic, or willing Inexperienced or unable	Forming
D2	Below average readiness Unconfident, insecure, or unwilling Inexperienced or unable	Storming
D3	Above average readiness Unconfident, insecure, or unwilling Experienced or able	Norming
D4	High readiness Confident, secure, and willing Experienced and able	Performing
D3	Above average readiness Unconfident, insecure, or unwilling Experienced or able	Adjourning

Note: Adapted from K. Blanchard, P. Zigarmi, & D. Zigarmi (1985), *Leadership and the One-Minute Manager,* New York: Morrow.

& Blanchard, 1982, 1996). The model suggests that the leadership style of the effective leader evolves from highly directive style to a more democratic one as the readiness and developmental level of followers increases over time. Both transactional and transformational outcomes can be achieved by selecting and delivering the appropriate skills noted in Chapter 4.

In the Hersey and Blanchard model, the amount of task direction and relationship support needed is dependent upon the readiness or developmental level of the followers in relation to a specific task. Table 5.2 describes the relationship between leadership style, follower readiness, and follower need level based on the revised model using Blanchard's developmental levels.

▼ LEADERSHIP STYLE AND GROUP STAGES

The Situational Leadership model matches a leadership style to each readiness or developmental level (Hersey & Blanchard, 1982). The directing or telling style (S1) is appropriate for groups or individuals

TABLE 5.2 *Relationship Between Leadership Style, Readiness, and Need Level*

Leadership Style	Style Description	Readiness	Need Level
Directing (S1)	High task and low relationship	Inexperienced and willing (R1)	Physiological needs, security needs
Coaching (S2)	High task and high relationship	Inexperienced and unwilling (R2)	Belonging and social needs
Supporting (S3)	Low task and high relationship	Experienced and unwilling or unconfident (R3)	Recognition and esteem needs
Delegating (S4)	Low task and low relationship	Experienced and willing (R4)	Achievement and higher needs

Note: Adapted from P. Hersey & K. H. Blanchard (1982), *Management of Organizational Behavior: Utilizing Human Resources* (4th ed.), Englewood Cliffs, NJ: Prentice-Hall, and K. H. Blanchard (1984), *Situational Leadership* II, Escondido, CA: Blanchard Training and Development.

with low readiness levels and is best described as high task, low relationship. The coaching or selling style (S2) works best with below average readiness levels and is high task, high relationship. The supporting or participating style (S3) should be paired with above average readiness levels and is low task, high relationship. Finally, the delegating style (S4), characterized as low task, low relationship works best with individuals and groups with high readiness levels.

The four leadership styles described in the Situational Leadership model can be directly related to the stages of group development (Carew, et al. 1990; Kormanski, 1985). When working with individuals, the styles flow progressively, one into another, as the individuals increase in readiness. The same pattern occurs with groups and teams. Leading in this context involves assessing the readiness of the group instead of the individual and delivering the matching style to the group as a unit.

Even though the members of a group or team may vary in terms of their readiness to carry out a particular task, the leader should assess the readiness of the group as a whole to complete the task. The leader of a company team that will carry out a charity fund-raising project assessed his team at readiness level R3 (experienced and unwilling) (see Table 5.2). The members were experienced and had previously participated in similar efforts, but most had restrictions on the amount of time they could contribute, making them somewhat unwilling. Other readiness levels were present in a few individuals, but as a team they were best categorized as readiness level 3 and required a supporting/ participating leadership style, which is low task, high relationship.

The model also works regressively. When an individual or group encounters a crisis, readiness decreases and the leader needs to move backward to the previous style. The adjourning stage, for example, creates such a crisis and requires this type of adjustment. It must be borne in mind that crises not only occur in the workplace (a more likely happening for groups); but they may also happen elsewhere and be brought to the work site (a more likely happening for individuals).

Consider again the team just described, which the leader assessed at readiness level 3 in relation to the task of raising funds for a charity. As noted, the leader planned to use a supporting/participating style of leadership. However, if a crisis occurs, such as difficulty in selecting a meeting time, he will increase his directive behavior and regress back to a coaching style (S2) of high task, high relationship.

When the natural pattern of group development is integrated with the Situational Leadership model the directing style is correlated with the forming stage, the coaching style is matched with the storming stage, the supporting style is paired with the norming stage, the delegating style is used during the performing stage, and there is a regression back to the supporting style for the adjourning stage (Kormanski, 1985).

Returning to the charity fund-raising team, although the team leader planned to use a supportive, participating style most of the time, he would briefly use a directive style (high task, low relationship) initially to structure the task and resolve dependency issues. He planned to use a coaching style next (high task, high relationship) as the team discussed a process for task completion, since he expected there to be some healthy conflict during the discussion. Most of the time, however, he would use leadership styles 3 (supporting/participating) and 4 (delegating). The team, which he had assessed at a readiness level of 3, should be receptive to this plan.

The natural process of group development encourages movement toward the third and fourth stages, which result in cooperative productivity. But the early stages are developmental prerequisites and, thus, are necessary. The leader should be sure the group remains in them long enough to resolve growth issues and should assist the members by using the appropriate leadership styles. Thus, both directing and coaching are short-term styles. The high task style of directing can be used only for a short time because of its low relationship component. Although this style is effective in the forming stage of a group, individuals prefer to experience more relationship behavior in the workplace and become frustrated if it is absent for long periods of time. The coaching style, too, is short term, because it requires the leader to provide both high task and high relationship direction during a time of member resistance and hostility (the storming stage). To provide such direction over a long period of time would result in professional burnout. The following sections examine more closely the interaction between leadership style and group stage. Table 5.3 summarizes the concepts that are discussed.

TABLE 5.3 *Relationship Between Group Development Stage, Leadership Style, and Readiness/Development Level*

Group Development Stage	Leadership Style	Team Readiness/ Developmental Level
1. Forming	High task and low relationship	Low readiness Eager, enthusiastic, or willing Inexperienced or unable
2. Storming	High task and high relationship	Below average readiness Unconfident, insecure, or unwilling Inexperienced or unable
3. Norming	Low task and high relationship	Above average readiness Unconfident, insecure, or unwilling Experienced or able
4. Performing	Low task and low relationship	High readiness Confident, secure, and willing Experienced or able
5. Adjourning	Low task and high relationship	Above average readiness Unconfident, insecure, or unwilling Experienced or able

Note: Adapted from K. H. Blanchard (1984), *Situational Leadership II*, Escondido, CA: Blanchard Training and Development.

Directing and Forming

Style 1 of the Situational Leadership model is a highly directive approach involving high task, low relationship behavior. It is most effective with groups that have low readiness, that is, groups that are unable but willing to carry out the task in question. For completion of the group's task, these are the most dangerous type of group members. Their eagerness and enthusiasm combined with their inexperience may cause them to go where angels fear to tread. The leader's high task behavior involves stating expectations and standards clearly, providing an instructional component, and supervising very closely. The leader implements low relationship behavior by being professional and friendly. As good performance occurs, relationship behavior is increased. Catching people doing something right and praising them is a good example of this strategy (Blanchard & Johnson, 1982). Because this style is leader centered, it is called directing.

The forming stage (stage 1) of group development is characterized by low task-relevant readiness. An analysis of group interaction at this stage would reveal a major concern with resolving inclusion issues (Schutz, 1958); behavior that is individually centered (Thelen & Dickerman, 1949); individual members who are rated low on task ability (Bales, 1958); dependent and, thus, unreliable membership patterns (Bennis & Shepard, 1956); and member requests and statements concerning orientation (Bales, 1953). A strong need for security is a key motivator for the group members. Maslow's (1954) hierarchy of needs is in evidence, as members of the group demonstrate the need for safety, security, and nurturance.

By using a highly directive and structured style, the leader provides a means of resolving dependency relationships and orienting group members to the task at hand (Kormanski, 1985). Inexperienced followers need instruction and supervision conducted in a friendly, professional manner. Willing followers need clear standards and expectations followed by praise and encouragement as they learn and perform.

Coaching and Storming

Style 2 of the Situational Leadership model includes both high task and high relationship behaviors and is most effective with followers or groups that are inexperienced and unwilling. Leaders find this group of followers the most difficult to work with. They must provide high task direction, clarifying tasks, explaining the rationale behind tasks, and encouraging questioning from the followers or group. In addition, they need to use high relationship behavior to combat the increasing unwillingness of the group members. Once the orientation period is over and dependency issues are resolved, group members often do not want to do things in the way in which they were instructed and find many tasks more complicated than they thought they would be. Personality differences are heightened, and it is not uncommon for members to attack the leadership during this time. With a high task, high relationship style, the leader can focus increased attention on members' frustration (high relationship) while maintaining an effort to reduce dissatisfaction (high task). These strategies provide opportunities for understanding, active listening, and praise for good performance. The style is called coaching because the leader is the experienced expert and must coach the inexperienced, somewhat resistant followers.

The storming stage (stage 2) of group development is characterized by various degrees of conflict and emotions. Behavioral patterns are counterdependent (Bennis & Shepard, 1956) and involve frustration (Thelen & Dickerman, 1949), testing (Mills, 1964), and control issues (Schutz, 1958). Underlying this volatile stage is the members' need to belong and their desire for increased social interaction (Maslow, 1954).

The conflict that occurs during the storming stage makes this stage the most critical one in the group's development. It is essential for the leader to manage the conflict effectively in order to provide opportunity for subsequent growth (Kormanski, 1982). Interventions during this stage require both high task and high relationship behaviors. The leader must assume an active and directive posture but also must directly involve the group members by explaining decisions and providing opportunities for clarification (Hersey & Blanchard, 1982).

Supporting and Norming

Style 3 consists of low task and high relationship behaviors. This style matches the needs of a group that is above average in readiness level but is still somewhat unwilling to assume total responsibility for the task. For the leader, this group of followers is often the most disappointing. However, the unwillingness the group members show often results from a lack of confidence rather than from any negative feelings regarding the task itself. Also, time management issues may arise in this stage that force choices, resulting in unwillingness on the part of the group members. The leader must maintain high supportive relationship behaviors to combat the group's unwillingness and lack of confidence. By reducing the amount of directive task behavior, the leader allows the group to assume increased task responsibility. Because this leadership style involves two-way communication about the task, shared decision making, and strong encouragement, it is called supporting.

The norming stage (stage 3) of group development is marked by a move toward group unity, with an emphasis on openness (Schutz, 1982), morale (Slater, 1966), and harmony (Miles, 1981). Increased member participation is evidenced by the encouragement of confrontation (Mann, 1967), integration (Hare, 1976), and involvement (Miles, 1981). Individuals at this stage frequently rate their activity and task ability high (Bales, 1958). Underlying the behavior evidenced in this stage is the need for esteem and recognition (Maslow, 1954).

The evolution of the norming stage is enhanced when a participating style of leadership is used. The high relationship behavior of the leader contributes to the development of cohesion, while his or her low task behavior encourages the expression of opinions and increases open communication. The goal of cooperation is perceived by all as realistic and reachable. The leader's role now includes sharing ideas, facilitating decision making and problem solving (Hersey & Blanchard, 1982), and providing feedback and socioemotional support. There is a developmental aspect to this stage, too. As the group becomes more confident and more willing to assume responsibility for directing its own operations, the leader can begin to reduce supportive behaviors (Kormanski, 1985).

Delegating and Performing

Leadership style 4, which involves both low task and low relationship behaviors, is most effective with groups with high task readiness. The members of such groups are both experienced and willing as a result of their ongoing development; they do not need or expect the task-directive behaviors or the socioemotional support and consultative behaviors that the leader has provided in the past. They are competent, confident, and highly motivated. For the leader, they are the most delightful and desirable followers. Because the task is, in effect, now turned over to the group, the leader's style is termed delegating. Delegating provides the opportunity for group self-motivation and self-direction with regard to task accomplishment. The members of the group are able to set challenging but realistic goals and to utilize pride as a motivating factor. They need minimum supervision and, in fact, may regard more than a minimum level of task or relationship behavior from the leader as interference or evidence of a lack of trust in their abilities. However, although the leader's task and relationship behaviors are reduced significantly, they are not eliminated completely. The leader still must maintain open channels of communication to provide for pertinent interchanges of task-relevant information. In addition, periodic reinforcement for outstanding achievement may be appropriate (Kormanski, 1985).

The performing stage (stage 4) of group development is characterized by a high level of group maturity, and group behavior is focused on goal attainment (Hare, 1976) and internalization (Mann, 1967). Members show high task ability, activity, and likability (Bales, 1958). Self-actualization and the higher needs of Maslow (1954, 1971) along with McClelland's (1961) needs of achievement, affiliation, and power are the major sources of motivation.

Supporting the Adjournment Crisis

As noted earlier, the Situational Leadership model, although developmental in nature, is also regressive. A crisis often will result in a decrease in task readiness level. In such a situation, the leader would move backward to the preceding Situational Leadership style and delivery that matches the new readiness level (Kormanski, 1985).

Because concluding a group creates some apprehension and brings on a minor adjournment crisis, the readiness level of the group generally will regress. If the group has been responsible for its own functioning but now seems to be unable or unwilling to continue to do so, the appropriate leadership behavior would be to change to the supportive style (Kormanski, 1985). Because the adjourning stage of group development centers around separation, grieving and leaving behaviors are typical (Ward, 1982). The termination of the group is a regressive movement from giving up control to giving up inclusion in the group (Schutz, 1958).

The supporting style facilitates the task termination and disengagement process. The leader's low task behavior allows group members to become actively involved in the group's conclusion while his or her high relationship support helps to combat members' reluctance to leave and desire to remain within the safe, predictable structure of the group. If the crisis were to persist, the leader would match the decreasing task maturity level by regressing to the coaching style and increasing the amount of task directive behavior to achieve closure. Table 5.4 describes appropriate leader behaviors associated with each leadership style.

Styles and Stages Review

Both leadership styles 1 and 2 (directing and coaching) and group development stages 1 and 2 (forming and storming) are developmental in nature. The forming and storming stages provide opportunities for growth by involving group members in orientation, instruction, clarification, and supervision. This developmental process is supported by the leader's increased relationship behavior following good performance; encouragement to continue to gain experience; and provision of rewards for learning and improving skills. The relationship behavior of leadership style 1 is low but is increased as the group assumes more responsibility for a task. If it is not increased as the group matures, resentment may occur. Because leadership style 2 involves high levels of both task and relationship behavior, it requires a lot of time and effort on the part of the leader. The developmental aspect of style 2 encourages group members to become more involved in the task as their ability to perform the task increases, which necessitates increased

TABLE 5.4 *Behaviors Associated With Each Leadership Style*

Leadership Style	Leader Behaviors
Telling/Directing (S1)	Acts in a professional and friendly manner Provides concrete expectations Uses an instructional component Supervises performance closely
Selling/Coaching (S2)	Offers encouragement and rewards Provides opportunities for belonging Adds additional clarification of the task information Gives advice based on expertise
Participating/ Supporting (S3)	Provides opportunities for increased self-esteem Offers joint decision-making tasks Supports performance Shares data
Delegating (S4)	Provides essential task information Offers the opportunity for continuous communication Requests professional evaluation of tasks Encourages challenging performance goals

Note: Adapted from C. L. Kormanski (1996b), "Team Interventions: Moving the Team Forward," in J. W. Pfeiffer (Ed.), *The 1996 Annual: Volume 2, Consulting* (pp. 85–88), San Francisco: Pfeiffer & Co.

leader involvement as well. In addition, the leader is using the more time-consuming high relationship behaviors to deal with follower unwillingness. High transactional skills are needed at these readiness levels as well.

Leadership styles 3 and 4 (delegating and supporting) and group development stages 3 and 4 (norming and performing) are working styles. The norming and performing stages concentrate on cooperative productivity. Opportunities for collaborative efforts and team projects are encouraged and supported. Interdependence is stressed, and feelings of cohesiveness abound. Minimal task behavior is required of the leader. Further, the leader's relationship behavior in style 3 is decreased as the style is used. Thus, both styles 3 and 4 are time-efficient and preferred styles for the experience level of the followers. It is during the last three stages of group development that the leader delivers more transformational skills using leadership styles 3 and 4. Experienced followers are well suited to this increase in transformational leadership, and the result is a continuing dynamic work group. Table 5.5 summarizes the five stages of group development, their corresponding leadership styles, descriptions of the readiness level of the group, and the related need level based on Maslow's (1954, 1971) hierarchy of needs.

▼ LEADERSHIP STYLE AND POWER

The power bases for leadership change from position power to personal power sources as the individual or group increases in readiness (Hersey & Blanchard, 1982; Kormanski, 1988). Each of the seven power bases described in Chapter 4 can be useful in implementing one or more of the Situational Leadership styles (Hersey et al. 1979; Hersey & Blanchard, 1982; Kormanski, 1988).

Effective leaders develop power in all seven areas (Hersey & Blanchard, 1982). The power a leader possesses at a given time is also related to the follower's perception of that power. Inexperienced followers do not perceive expert power as having the same amount of influence as do experienced followers. Reward power also affects inexperienced and experienced followers very differently, with the former responding more quickly and frequently to this type of power than the latter (Hersey & Blanchard, 1982). Position power bases are related to a directive style and are most effective with low readiness individuals (Hersey & Blanchard, 1982; Kormanski, 1988). Personal power bases are related to democratic leadership styles and are preferred by experienced group members (Cummings, 1981; McAfee & Champagne, 1987). Group development stages follow the same pattern, with the

TABLE 5.5 *Relationship Between Group Development Stage, Leadership Style, Readiness Level, And Individual Needs*

Group Development Stage	Leadership Style	Team Readiness Level	Team Members' Individual Needs
1. Forming	Directing or Telling (S1)	Low readiness Eager, enthusiastic, or willing Inexperienced or unable (D1, R1, M1)	Physiological needs, safety and security needs
2. Storming	Coaching or Selling (S2)	Below average readiness Unconfident, insecure, or unwilling Inexperienced or unable (D1, R1, M2)	Belonging and social needs
3. Norming	Supporting or Participating (S3)	Above average readiness Unconfident, insecure, or unwilling Experienced or able (D1, R1, M3)	Recognition and esteem needs
4. Performing	Delegating (S4)	High readiness Confident, secure, and willing Experienced and able (D1, R1, M4)	Self-actualization and higher needs
5. Adjourning	Supporting or Participating (S3)	Above average readiness Unconfident, insecure, or unwilling Experienced or able (D1, R1, M3)	Recognition and esteem needs

Note: Adapted from P. Hersey & K. H. Blanchard (1982), *Management of Organizational Behavior: Utilizing Human Resources* (4th ed.), Englewood Cliffs, NJ: Prentice-Hall, and K. H. Blanchard (1984), Situational Leadership II, Escondido, CA: Blanchard Training and Development.

early stages of forming and storming requiring position power bases and the later stages of norming, performing, and adjourning demanding the personal power bases.

Initial thinking regarding the relationship of power bases to the Situational Leadership styles suggested a hierarchy from the position power bases of coercive, connective, reward, and legitimate power to the personal power bases of referent, informational, and expert power (Hersey & Blanchard, 1982). With the reversal of the task maturity description for the initial level from unwilling to willing in Blanchard's Situational Leadership II model, a rethinking of this relationship is in order. The following reorganization appears to fit current trends and is summarized in Table 5.6.

TABLE 5.6 *Relationship Between Group Development Stage, Leadership Style, and Power Bases*

Group Development Stage	Leadership Style	Power Bases
1. Forming	High task, low relationship	Reward, Connective
2. Storming	High task, high relationship	Legitimate, Connective
3. Norming	Low task, high relationship	Referent, Informational
4. Performing	Low task, low relationship	Expert, Informational
5. Adjourning	Low task, high relationship	Referent, Informational

Note: Adapted from P. Hersey, K. H. Blanchard, & W. E. Natemeyer (1979), "Situational Leadership, Perception, and the Impact of Power," *Group and Organizational Studies, 4,* 418–428.

Forming With Reward Power

During the forming stage of group development, a high task, low relationship directive style is most appropriate for leading willing and inexperienced followers. A reward power base is essential, as the progressive nature of the model requires increasing relationship behavior. Reward power is also needed to follow the stating of expectations, the setting of standards, and the task instruction, as well as to accompany the close supervision provided by the directive style when good performance is exhibited. Poor performance requires a restating of expectations and standards and further instruction.

Storming With Legitimate Power

As the storming stage evolves and unwillingness combines with inexperience, a high task, high relationship coaching style is needed. A legitimate power base is important for defining roles and regulations, implementing contract agreements, and maintaining standard operating procedures. The legitimate power base sets limits that help keep the conflict contained and allow for conflict management interventions. This power base also assists in clarifying tasks, offering rewards, and providing opportunities for belonging. Weisbord (1987) described the work of the Emery pioneers in the development of large group organizational change processes in Australia, a highly unionized country, and suggested that they believed that gaining the legal right to control and coordinate work would render group, interpersonal, and communications techniques unnecessary. Although the latter part of this belief seems highly unlikely in an experienced contemporary workforce, it is more likely in a less experienced workforce. The legal right to control and coordinate work is a type of legitimate power. This power base contributes to the coaching style, which involves the leaders selling expert advice to inexperienced followers. Legitimate power directly combats the unwillingness characteristic of the storming stage of group development.

Norming With Referent Power

At the start of the norming stage, followers are still somewhat unwilling or unconfident though they have gained experience. A low task, high relationship supporting style is best suited for this situation, since experienced people do not need a high task focus and the high relationship behavior challenges their unwillingness. Experienced followers are more influenced by a referent power base which relies on trust, loyalty, openness, and interpersonal relationships, than by position power bases. Referent power is also useful in combating the followers' unwillingness and building their confidence. This change from position power to personal power places more emphasis on the personality of the leader. The supporting style with the referent power base stresses joint decision making, opportunities for building self-esteem, shared data, and supported performance.

Performing With Expert Power

As the performing stage begins and followers become more willing as well as experienced, the low task, low relationship delegating style is used. The leader must now depend more on the expert power base, which involves the possession of expertise, skill, and knowledge. Respect for the leader and the pride of the followers are also important ingredients that undergird the influence of the expert power base. The delegating style uses this influence to provide essential task information, encourage challenging performance goals, maintain open communication channels, and utilize the follower to provide task evaluation data. Finally, people with high readiness have a strong preference for performance feedback, which experts can provide.

Adjourning With Referent Power

The adjourning stage of group development requires a regressive movement back to the supporting leadership style, which uses a referent power base. As tasks are completed and/or the group begins to disband, the low task, high relationship style assists group members to separate from the work and disengage from relationships. The referent power of the leader aids in facilitating the process by using personal traits to create ceremonies, rituals, and structured ways of bringing closure.

Connective and Informational Power

Two lesser power bases that have recently been discussed in the literature support the four major power bases presented with the group development stages. Connective power supports reward and legitimate power, the two major position power bases, and is used with inexperienced group members. It emphasizes the leader's connections with influential people inside and outside the organization. A key relationship is the one with the leader's immediate supervisor.

Informational power supports referent and expert power, the other personal power bases, and is used with experienced group members. It emphasizes the leader's possession of or access to information that is perceived by others as valuable. A key source of information is the informal communication network within an organization. Table 5.6 summarizes the relationship between group development stages, leadership styles, and power bases.

Coercive power

Coercive power is based upon fear and the ability to punish. This power base is fast losing its prominence in the workplace. It is being replaced as a major power base by legitimate power, as today there is more reliance on contracts, federal regulations for equal opportunity employment, and standardized operating procedures. Initially, coercive power was related to the high task, low relationship style of leadership (Hersey & Blanchard, 1982; Kormanski, 1988). However, the revised description of the readiness levels in the Situational Leadership II model (Blanchard et al., 1985) would suggest reward power as a more appropriate base for interacting with willing employees. The use of coercive power with unwilling, inexperienced individuals that is noted in the original theory is now suspect because of the changing times and the current emphasis on participative management. Indeed, coercive power has always been a volatile power source with a high degree of unpredictability and the ability to create highly emotional atmospheres. At times, however, it has been the only solution for assuring the survival of a particular work group or organization.

Coercive power should be used sparingly and as a last resort. Therefore, it is not very useful with a specific group development stage or leadership style. Furthermore, when using coercive power, one should follow the guidelines proposed in many psychology texts concerning the use of discipline by parents. The analogy of parents disciplining their children is an excellent one for understanding why coercive power is sometimes necessary and for understanding the ways in which it can be abused. The guidelines for the use of coercive power are as follows:

▼ punish the behavior not the people;
▼ punishment should be fair and just;
▼ punishment should be short;
▼ punishment should closely follow the behavior;
▼ alternative behavior should be offered to avoid punishment
▼ punishment should be used sparingly and not impulsively.

It should be noted that Blanchard and Johnson's (1982) 1-minute reprimand is not a form of coercive power but is a feedback mechanism that reminds experienced employees about quality and standards. Blanchard and Johnson suggested that if the employees are inexperienced, they need instruction, not reprimands. Although the 1-minute reprimand follows the guidelines of discipline, it also includes a focus on feelings and ends with a 1-minute praise for the person, as it is the behavior and not the person that is the focus of the reprimand.

▼ APPLICATIONS FOR TASK GROUPS

Gable and Kormanski (1983) described how the Situational Leadership model was used to assist a branch office manager of a brokerage firm. This manager, like most in the firm, was promoted to that position from the sales force. The basic leadership style that salespeople in the firm used with clients was the high task, high relationship coaching style, which is a strong selling style. A secondary style that they used with clients with experience was the supporting style. Rarely did they use the directing or the delegating style.

Because the manager oversaw not only the sales force, which itself was composed of a variety of individuals, but also an office of clerical, secretarial, and janitorial personnel, he needed to use all of the leadership styles, not just the coaching and supporting styles. In addition, he had limited control over the income of the sales force, which operated largely on commission. The salespeople were to an extent in business for themselves and maintained their own clientele. They tended to have a greater degree of independence than subordinates in other managerial situations.

An early suggestion made to the manager was to use a directing style for new employees and sales trainees instead of using a coaching style for everyone. Another suggestion was to use the supporting and delegating styles with employees who had years of service with the firm and were experienced in doing the day-to-day tasks. The insight that the constant use of the high task, high relationship coaching style was contributing to feelings of burnout also encouraged the use of a variety of styles.

A valuable insight was also achieved regarding sales meetings. Since a variety of readiness levels were represented at the meetings, the agenda content could not be too simple or too complex. Content that was too simple would bore experienced veterans, and content that was too complex would confuse the recent additions to the sales staff. The veteran staff members needed the communication channel the meetings provided to keep current and to exchange information with their manager, and the new staff members received a major portion of their professional development and training in this setting.

Using Situational Leadership concepts, an alternate structure was created that consisted, in part, of regularly scheduled sales meetings that were limited to administrative communications and the exchange of brief verbal summaries of sales ideas among the sales staff. The goal was to stimulate new members without boring veterans. In addition, the manager divided the sales staff into an inexperienced group and an experienced group based on their knowledge of the system and sales productivity. He met with the inexperienced group on a regular basis for professional development (i.e., product knowledge, selling skills, time management), and during these meetings he used the directing and coaching styles. He met separately with the experienced group as needed to discuss topics of mutual interest, to allow for their input, and to engage them in selected joint decision-making activities; during these meetings he used the supporting and delegating styles.

Ward (1982) advocated the use of a democratic leadership style to allow and encourage the individual interaction necessary for group development and eventual shared leadership. The application of the Situational Leadership model to group development suggests that this style would work best during the latter stages of group life (norming, performing, and adjourning) and would not be effective during the early stages (forming and storming). Fiedler (1967) suggested that a democratic style of leadership is most appropriate for moderately structured groups and that highly unstructured and highly structured groups profit most from a directive style of leadership.

Their research and that of others suggests that as a group is forming and is uncommitted and uncertain of itself and its task, a more directive style provides instruction, direction, and structure. During the storming stage, when group members question things, ask for clarification, and begin to develop trust, the coaching style encourages individual involvement and reinforces performance while still providing some direction and impetus to the group's activities.

As group members gain experience in working together and in working on the task at hand and are able to handle more responsibility, a more democratic style of leadership can be used (Hersey & Blanchard, 1982). The supporting and delegating styles provide opportunities for group members to experience shared and democratic leadership. Eventually, even supportive relationship behavior from the leader is reduced as it is replaced by individual pride and self-motivation. As termination of the group approaches and the crisis of separation ensues, the leader's supportive relationship behavior again is increased to help the group deal with termination issues.

As a group moves through the stages of development, the leader is constantly defining tasks, assessing readiness, matching a leadership style to readiness level, delivering the style, and evaluating the outcome (Hersey & Blanchard, 1982). This process occurs within four leader/follower dimensions. The leader is responsible for a project (the macro task dimension) that is to be completed by the group (the macro relationship dimension). To accomplish this project, individuals (the micro relationship dimension) are assigned specific tasks (the micro task dimension). Leadership can be very complex at times.

In addition to assessing readiness, it is helpful for the leader to assess both group and individual motivation levels. Further, when choosing a leadership style, mobilizing the appropriate power bases is critical. As the style is delivered, choosing the right mix of transacting and transforming skills is important for continued growth and survival of the group.

Understanding group development and its naturally occurring stages provides insight for effective leader interventions. It also offers a diagnostic basis for analyzing group malfunctions and group disintegration. From a prediction standpoint, the group development model offers the leader an opportunity to develop realistic expectations concerning group process and group outcomes. Finally, it offers a road map of a normal pattern of development that can be utilized to assess progress.

Zimpfer (1986) reviewed a planning process for using knowledge about group development stages that can be implemented by those in leadership roles. He examined counseling and therapy groups, encounter and personal growth groups, and training and self-analytic groups. Six specific applications were noted:

▼ choosing an appropriate theory or model;
▼ diagnosing group progress and achievement;
▼ diagnosing individual member growth;
▼ overcoming barriers to group development;
▼ providing a clearer view of termination; and
▼ suggesting tools and techniques to determine progress.

Zimpfer suggested that these applications are most fitting for small groups that have a stable membership and a specified goal or task. He also noted that the model would not be readily applicable to highly structured groups or to groups with limited opportunity for involvement, infrequent meetings, or a short time duration. Although the groups Zimpfer discussed were not task groups, the specific applications relate directly to work teams.

Donigian and Malnati (1987) noted two important components of training for group therapists. The cognitive component provides information that will help future therapists anticipate and predict group events and critical incidents. The experiential component is necessary for recognition and illumination of group process. Both contribute to a more realistic understanding of group development.

Yalom (1985) listed 11 curative factors available to individuals in the group setting. These include the following:

▼ instillation of hope;
▼ universality (I'm not the only one with this problem);
▼ catharsis (emotional expressions);
▼ corrective recapitulation of the primary family group (family reenactment);
▼ group cohesiveness;
▼ altruism (concern for others);
▼ interpersonal learning;
▼ imitative behavior (identification);
▼ imparting of information (guidance);
▼ development of socializing techniques; and
▼ existential factors (life is finite).

Group leaders can use group development concepts to increase the likelihood that group members might profit from these curative factors. Waldo (1985) suggested that the factors are robust enough to encompass the concerns addressed by contemporary groups. Although this research addressed counseling and therapy settings, there appears to be some general insight that pertains to all groups and teams in a variety of settings.

Weber (1982) used a human life analogy to describe the life stages of a group, comparing the life of a group to the life of an individual. He examined group behavior, group task issues, group interpersonal issues, and leadership issues. He likened the forming stage to infancy; the storming stage to adolescence; and the norming and performing stages to adulthood (young and mature levels). Although not specifically mentioned, the adjourning stage would be elder adulthood.

Winston, Boney, Miller, and Dagley (1988) described an intentionally structured group that is an intervention designed to promote specific goals. Created to promote student development on the college campus, this type of group occurs in a planned social environment, has set goals, is designed to promote human development, and has specified rules that maintain the essential structure. The group leader assumes major responsibility for both content and process. Behavior change and learning evolve from the dynamics from the group interaction. A planned structure is purposefully used to maximize the efforts of psychological forces in promoting these objectives.

Winston et al. (1988) presented a model that divides groups into three categories based on the degree of structure, purpose, and desired outcomes. In the model, structure refers to the leader's control, the group goals, and the member roles. The more ambiguity present, the less structure in the group. Overall purpose can involve therapy, training, or development. Some groups may, however, overlap and include more than one purpose. Typical desired outcomes include information acquisition, personality change, skills development, attitude change, organizational change, and interpersonal effectiveness.

Schein (1985) described four phases of the life cycle of the organization. As an organization grows larger and more interactive, the way in which it is managed and the overall style of leadership changes in an evolutionary manner to adapt to this expansion and increase in complexity. If one views this developmental process over the years (or decades for some organizations), the broad pattern resembles the Situational Leadership model and the descriptions of behavioral themes within the organization mirror those of the group development stages.

The pattern begins when the organization is founded, and the first phase is best described as an autocracy. The founding individuals begin to hire employees and provide them with an orientation to the company. Dependency needs are high and the management style is very directive (high task, low relationship). As effective performance increases, management's relationship behavior increases resulting in growth and opportunity for expansion.

Expansion results in more employees and the need for supervisors as well as a set of standard operating procedures. Thus, the organization evolves into a bureaucracy. During this second phase, roles are defined, relationship behavior is increased, and the management style becomes a coaching one (high task, high relationship) with the experienced supervisors providing clarification and encouragement to combat the emergence of conflict.

As employees gain experience and expertise in the technology of the company, a consultative phase begins. Input from nonmanagement personnel is sought, and there is an increasing amount of shared decision making. An open flow of communication creates a more cooperative atmosphere, and feelings of unity and cohesion are apparent. A supportive management style (low task, high relationship) encourages increased participation by employees and provides both materialistic and nonmaterialistic rewards.

The final stage in Schein's model is a participative phase. It occurs as employees begin to share the leadership role. A spirit of interdependence and competence in problem solving are characteristic of the organization's behavior. The delegating style (low task, low relationship) of management provides opportunities for personal and professional employee growth as well as the freedom for new technological developments to be nurtured. Productivity is both efficient and effective.

Table 5.7 illustrates the relationship between Schein's organizational life cycle model, the Situational Leadership model, and group development stages. The behavioral fit is better than the terminology fit, as the names Schein gave to the model's third and fourth stages create some confusion. Schein's behavioral description of the third stage of organizational life suggests management-employee participation in decision making, but because employees are consulted, consultation was used to name the phase. Similarly, the fourth stage, which emphasizes the management style of delegation, is behaviorally consistent with consultation, but because both management and employees are involved in the process, the term participative was used to name the phase.

As a final point, it is important to remember that what has been written here about leadership behavior and organizational life will likely not be the final word. As new paradigms emerge, continued experimentation will lead to additional insights and suggest different approaches to influence organizational change. Let us not forget that change is a given and evolution does not have an ending point.

▼ DISCUSSION OF RELEVANT EXPERIENCES

As the team of Irma, Ron, Grace, and Alex continued to discuss leadership style, they contributed examples from their own experiences. Irma suggested that an understanding of the theory of group development and its implications for leadership behavior can be a valuable tool for the consultant, facilitator, or leader. The behavioral themes of each stage of group development offer insight into what happens naturally in a group; patterns that deviate from those themes suggest possible problems and a need for intervention. Such patterns might include moving too fast, skipping stages, focusing only on task dimensions, and blockages or fixations in particular stages.

Ron noted that a facilitator who is eager to accomplish as much as possible to impress his or her superiors may spend little or no time on the forming process (stage 1) in order to get directly to work on the task. Doing so, however, will undoubtedly result in confusion and misunderstandings among the team members, thus hindering both group development and task accomplishment. A team leader who dislikes dealing with conflict may make quick, authoritative interventions or delegate decisions to the team, thus abdicating his or her role in helping to manage the team's conflict. The team is likely to view such behavior as unreasonable as well as unhelpful. Similarly, a leader who is very task oriented may not be aware of relationship issues and may fail to deal at all with dependency or hostility early in the development of the group. The resulting work atmosphere would be one of independent, individual effort in a rigid, inflexible pattern. Conversely, if a leader works too hard at building relationships, the group will develop problems during the norming process (stage 3) because of the leader's need to seek consensus on minor details.

Grace pointed out that mismatches between the stage of group development and leadership style often create serious problems. A leader's reluctance to change styles, generally because he or she is

TABLE 5.7 *Relationship Between Group Development Stage, Situational Leadership Style, and the Organizational Life Cycle*

Group Developmental Stage	Developmental Readiness Level	Situational Leadership Style	Management Behavior	Organizational Life Cycle Phase
1. Forming	Inexperienced, willing	Directing, Telling	High task, low relationship	Autocracy
2. Storming	Inexperienced, unwilling	Coaching, Selling	High task, high relationship	Bureaucracy
3. Norming	Experienced, unwilling or unconfident	Supporting, Participating	Low task, high relationship	Consultative
4. Performing	Experienced, willing	Delegating	Low task, low relationship	Participative
5. Adjourning	Experienced, unwilling or unconfident	Supporting, Participating	Low task, high relationship	Consultative

Note: Adapted from K. H. Blanchard (1984), *Situational Leadership II,* Escondido, CA: Blanchard Training and Development, and E. H. Schein (1985), *Organizational Culture and Leadership,* San Francisco: Jossey-Bass.

comfortable with only one or two styles or has developed skill in using only one or two styles, limits the leader's effectiveness and the team's chances for success. For example, a supervisor who favors the participating style may have difficulty initiating teamwork. Although more experienced team members may assume responsibility, the more inexperienced ones will flounder or withdraw from team action unless more task direction is provided. While seeking the security of task direction, members of new teams are likely to perceive leader behavior that is highly relationship oriented as inappropriate; in fact, they may be suspicious of it.

Alex described a company CEO who had used the high task, directing style in establishing the firm. This style was very helpful to new project teams in their early stages. However, the CEO would not change his leadership style once the teams became more functional, and his domineering, crisis-oriented style did not allow for open discussion and true efforts at consensus. Low morale, apathy, resentment, and low productivity caused the teams to be disbanded prematurely. Alex then described an equally ineffective manager who, when encouraged to delegate more as her workforce became more cohesive and productive, delegated only those tasks that she personally disliked doing. As the team members began to perceive this, and especially as the manager forgot to check on progress and provide praise and rewards for superior work, tasks were not completed on time, nor were they done well.

Irma discussed how the adolescent summer camp experience provides an excellent example of group development theory, especially when the focus is on new campers. Once the decision to attend camp is made, the movement toward awareness begins. Brochures are reexamined and additional mailings bring more information about the week at camp. Rules, regulations, and helpful hints initiate the orientation process and clarify dependency boundaries. Reality sets in as all the campers arrive on-site at the beginning of the week and are assigned to their living quarters. The forming stage continues as leaders provide orientation information and conduct structured activities of a get-acquainted nature to reduce dependency. Willing but inexperienced campers are eager and enthusiastic. However, a few campers who have been forced by adults into this environment are not only inexperienced but also unwilling. The similarity to many beginning group experiences across a wide variety of settings is apparent.

The next few days add more reality. Things are not as rose colored as the campers had thought. Sleeping till noon is not permitted. The food leaves much to be desired. Hiking is hard work. There is not enough free time. And most feel that a lot of the other campers in the unit are either bullies or jerks. There is resistance to the schedule and hostility toward fellow campers and particularly toward certain leaders. Conflict is clearly evident; the storming stage has begun. Most new campers are still inexperienced and are now becoming unwilling. Behaviors and attitudes reflect both chaotic and apathetic extremes and result in unwanted, negative outcomes.

The following days provide increased opportunities for learning. As opinions are expressed, communication and understanding increase. Group projects and efforts bring group successes, which in turn build cohesion and feelings of unity. A movement toward cooperation characterizes the norming stage. The new campers gain experience. They become a part of the group. They are not just included, but they are wanted. They belong. They may still be a little unconfident, and their need for more time to attempt to do many things thoroughly may make them unwilling at times, but they are now experienced.

The last few days of the week usher in a movement toward productivity and begin the performing stage. The willing and experienced campers have forgotten that they were neophytes at the beginning of the week. They have learned to work as a unit. Common problems get solved; interdependent teamwork can be seen in contest participation and other competitive camp events. The campers have even learned how to lose gracefully.

The final day brings the crisis of separation and the adjourning stage. The termination of the camping week and the disengagement from newly made friends is a difficult one. The more successful the camp experience, the more difficult it is to leave. Everyone knows how to say good-bye, but no one wants to do it. A ritualistic closing ceremony is utilized by the camp staff to bring closure.

As their discussion concluded, the topic for the next session became clear to Irma, Ron, Grace, and Alex. Team building and team performance would build on the knowledge they had generated concerning group development, leadership, and leadership styles. The team quickly resolved issues of topic selection and a meeting date and concluded their meeting.

Team Building

A good manager's job is to keep the few people who hate you away from the few who are undecided!

—Casey Stengel

*G*race, Irma, Ron, and Alex met during the fall to discuss the topic of team building. Prior to the meeting each had sent their research summaries to the other team members. Grace had explored team development; Irma related group development to team building; Ron examined team development patterns; and Alex wrote about team leader interventions. Their research summaries follow.

▼ TEAM DEVELOPMENT

In dynamic, growth-oriented organizations, the teams that are formed are often temporary and may involve frequent changes in member composition. The assumption of a stable group working together for an extended period of time may not be valid in today's organizational settings. Therefore, traditional methods of team building and team development may need to be reexamined (Pokora & Briner, 1988). In 1958, Bales noted that it may be easier to change the whole group or team than to change individual components such as member roles one at a time. In 1982, Hersey and Blanchard suggested that organizations should hire a wide diversity of individuals as opposed to only those who fit a corporate image and should place increased emphasis on the team building process to increase effectiveness.

Sundstrom, DeMeuse, and Futrell's (1990) review of the research conducted over the past 10 years suggested that team development interventions have enhanced work group effectiveness in some circumstances. Their concept of group effectiveness went beyond production and included satisfaction of team members and the group's future prospects as a work unit. Thus, they combined team viability with performance to yield effectiveness. Their concept of team development involved both group structure and interpersonal relationships. The interventions, then, could be directed toward role definition, goal setting, problem solving, or the interpersonal processes. Their conclusion was that a compelling model of team development was not yet available and more action research was needed.

Organizations have been gradually increasing the use of both formal self-managed teams (Dumaine, 1990) and the informal "skunk works" type of team described by Peters and Waterman (1982) to accompany an overall team-oriented approach for management (Varney, 1989). All of these approaches are contributing to the development of the superteam concept. Superteams stress achievement motivation, flexibility, networking, innovativeness, open communication channels, and an action orientation (Hastings, Bixby, & Chaudhry-Lawton, 1987). Although there is a strong reliance on transformational skills (e.g., flexibility, networking, and innovative thinking), the transactional skills are also in evidence (e.g., goal setting, communication, and problem solving).

Work teams are beginning to be viewed as the heart of the organization (Huszczo, 1990), and training in building and maintaining teams is becoming increasingly important to organizational management. Working together as a team does not always come naturally to every person, nor do all individuals bring the same amount of team experience to the workplace. Until recently, men had a distinct advantage by having had more team experience opportunities during their developmental years in activities such as athletics, youth groups, and summer camps. These activities provided an introduction to both the team experience and team leadership. Now women also bring such experiences to the workplace.

The success of teams rests on four critical components. First, there must be an organizational fit between the team and the mission and purpose of the organization. Second, effective leadership, either individual or shared, must be present. Third, team members must understand their roles and responsibilities. Fourth, the team must possess or have the potential talents to develop the resources needed to accomplish its assignments.

Effective team leadership requires the competencies described in each of the preceding chapters of this book. Effective leaders understand the nature and characteristics of the relationship between groups and teams (Chapter 1); the process of group development (Chapter 2); the dynamics of change and conflict (Chapter 3); the knowledge, skills, power, and motivation required for leadership (Chapter 4); and the interaction of follower and leadership style (Chapter 5).

Teams are most effective when they are matched to assignments based on readiness. A similar conclusion was reached by Hersey and

Blanchard (1982) for individuals in their Situational Leadership model to develop inexperienced employees. Not only must leadership style change as readiness increases, but more challenging assignments can be made as talents are developed and tasks are completed. Care should be given to assure that the team has adequate resources as well.

A few cautions are in order when considering training in team building. King (1989), upon interviewing several training consultants, concluded that ineffective leadership is a key cause of team failure. She described specifically two types of ineffective teams: hierarchical teams, in which members spend most of their time following a highly directive leader with limited team interaction opportunities, and circular teams, which emphasize harmony and avoid conflict. The former situation results from a leader staying too long in the forming stage and using a high task style; the latter results from a leader who skips the storming stage and uses a high relationship style. Huszczo (1990) identified the following common pitfalls to avoid when training teams:

▼ Confusing team building with teamwork;

▼ Viewing teams as if they are "closed systems";

▼ Not using a systematic model to plan team development;

▼ Starting team training without assessing team needs;

▼ Sending team members to team training individually rather than collectively;

▼ Treating team building as a Japanese management technique;

▼ Assuming that teams are all basically alike;

▼ Counting on training alone to develop effective teams;

▼ Treating team building as a program rather than a process; and

▼ Not holding teams accountable for using what they learn in team training.

In a similar vein, Varney (1989) stressed the need to constantly monitor team interaction, recognize habitual patterns that hinder productivity, and take appropriate corrective action.

Katherine Cole Esty (1987, p. 80) stated, "The best way to make training 'stick,' I believe, is to train teams of employees within an organization. Even a single team enhances the likelihood that the training will carry over and change the organization to some degree." The increasing attention given to the use of teams in organizational settings underscores the value of this technique as a strategy to combat increasing complexity and control change. Although generally favored, a team approach is infrequently instituted as an organization-wide program (Dyer, 1987). Kolb, Rubin, and McIntyre (1984) noted that the need for a team approach increases as one moves up the corporate hierarchy, where tasks become less structured and solutions less routine. It has also been noted that as the individual at all levels of the organization has less impact, the need for team effort becomes more crucial (Hellriegel et al., 1986; Kormanski & Mozenter, 1987).

Dumaine (1990) described the new superteam as a self-managed group consisting of 3 to 30 workers spanning a number of hierarchical levels and functions in an organization. He cited a recent survey of 476 top Fortune 1,000 companies that showed that while only 7% of the workforce was currently using self-managed teams, 50% of the companies surveyed planned to use them in the next few years. As one example, Dumaine noted that productivity had risen 40% since a team approach was begun at General Mills. Similar changes were seen at Federal Express, 3M, and Chaparral Steel, among others.

The need for team building is apparent. Solomon (1977, p. 181) stated, "Team building implies the ultimate purpose of increasing the effectiveness and efficiency of a group in its pursuit of personal and organizational objective." Pokora and Briner (1988) noted that team formation encourages the generation of ideas and energies from different parts of the organization to be used in developing new methods of operation. However, the team building process requires strong training skills, and the potential exists for either positive or negative outcomes (Woodcock & Francis, 1981).

▼ GROUP DEVELOPMENT AND TEAM BUILDING

Knowledge about the process of group development can easily be applied to team development, since all teams are groups. Hanson and

Lubin (1988) offered an overview of team building that related the process to group development. Their focus was on team characteristics and assessing the need for and conditions conducive to team development. They also described the role of the consultant in the team building process. Fay and Doyle (1982) suggested some specific characteristics drawn from group development theories that are applicable to team building. The following list groups characteristics of teams according to stage of group development and provides a set of guidelines for team leaders and facilitators.

STAGE 1: FORMING

▼ Members discover what behaviors are acceptable to the group;
▼ Transition from individual to member status occurs;
▼ Testing behavior is exhibited;
▼ Members show dependence on formal and informal group leadership for guidance in a newly unstructured environment;
▼ Attempts are made to identify tasks in terms of relevant parameters and to decide how the group will accomplish the task;
▼ Decisions are made on the type of information needed and how it will be used;
▼ Members are hesitant to participate;
▼ Members and leader test behavioral expectations and ways to handle behavioral problems;
▼ Members begin to feel attachment to the team;
▼ Intellectualizing occurs;
▼ Members discuss symptoms or problems peripheral to the task;
▼ Complaints are raised about the organizational environment;
▼ Suspicion, fear, and anxiety are expressed about the new situations; and
▼ Minimal work is accomplished.

STAGE 2: STORMING

▼ Members use hostility or overzealousness as a way to express their individuality;

- ▼ Members resist group formation;
- ▼ Members recognize the extent of the task demands;
- ▼ Members respond emotionally to the perceived requirements for self-change and self-denial;
- ▼ Infighting, defensiveness, and competition are evident;
- ▼ Members establish unachievable goals;
- ▼ Disunity, increased tension, and jealousy are evident;
- ▼ Members resist the task demands because they perceive them to interfere with personal needs;
- ▼ Polarization of group members occurs;
- ▼ Sharp fluctuations of relationships and reversals of feelings are seen;
- ▼ Concern is expressed over excessive work;
- ▼ Pecking orders are established; and
- ▼ Minimal work is accomplished.

STAGE 3: NORMING

- ▼ Members accept the team, team norms, their own roles, and the idiosyncrasies of fellow members;
- ▼ Emotional conflict is reduced by members' patching up previously conflicting relationships;
- ▼ Members attempt to achieve maximum harmony by avoiding conflict;
- ▼ A high level of intimacy is evident, characterized by members confiding in one another, sharing personal problems, and discussing team dynamics;
- ▼ Members show new ability to express emotions constructively;
- ▼ A sense of team cohesiveness, with a common spirit and goals is apparent;
- ▼ Team boundaries are established and maintained; and
- ▼ Moderate work is accomplished.

STAGE 4: PERFORMING

- ▼ The team becomes an entity capable of diagnosing and solving problems and making decisions;

▼ Members experience insight into personal and interpersonal processes;

▼ Constructive self-change is undertaken; and

▼ A great deal of work is accomplished.

STAGE 5: ADJOURNING

▼ Members express the need for revitalization;

▼ Members are ready to celebrate accomplishments;

▼ The team recycles to the forming stage when given new tasks;

▼ Leader intervention is necessary when the group is to disband; and

▼ Members have difficulty leaving successful group experiences.

Kormanski and Mozenter (1987) developed a team building model that is compatible with group development theory and emphasizes measurable task and relationship outcomes at each stage. As groups become teams, shared goals and commitment lead to an interdependent working relationship that results in achievement and pride for both the team and the organization (Hellriegel et al., 1986). The Kormanski/Mozenter model stresses group dynamics, behavioral themes, measurable outcomes, and performance feedback using team member ratings.

During the forming stage, groups begin to become teams as the task outcome of commitment to group goals and the relationship outcome of acceptance of other team members are obtained (Cascio, 1986; McGregor, 1960; Reese & Brandt, 1987). The process of becoming a team is further enhanced when there is congruence with and accountability to organizational goals (McAfee & Champagne, 1987; McGregor, 1960; Reese & Brandt, 1987; Reilly & Jones, 1974; Woodcock, 1979; Woodcock & Francis, 1981). During the storming stage, clarification of team purpose and direction by acknowledging and confronting conflict becomes the task outcome. The relationship outcome of belonging involves listening with understanding (Cascio, 1986; Francis & Young, 1979; McAfee & Champagne, 1987; McGregor, 1960; Reese & Brandt, 1987; Woodcock, 1979; Woodcock & Francis, 1981).

Team outcomes for the norming stage are, at the task level, involvement through shared decision making and, at the relationship level, support through respecting individual differences (Cascio, 1986; Dyer, 1987; Hellriegel et al., 1986; Woodcock & Francis, 1981). The performing stage focuses on the task outcome of achievement and the relationship outcome of pride (Dyer, 1987; Hellriegel et al., 1986; McAfee & Champagne, 1987; Woodcock & Francis, 1981). Finally, the adjourning stage outcomes are recognition at the task level and satisfaction at the relationship level (Dyer, 1987; Hellriegel et al., 1986; McAfee & Champagne, 1987; Reese & Brandt, 1987). Table 6.1 illustrates the integration of group development stages and team building outcomes.

The Team Development Rating Scale developed by Kormanski and Mozenter (1987) is based upon stage theories of group development. Each stage (forming, storming, norming, performing, and adjourning) is represented by a task dimension and a relationship dimension (Tuckman, 1965; Tuckman & Jensen, 1977). Two performance outcomes are provided for each stage, one to assess task behaviors (the odd-numbered items) and one to assess relationship behaviors (the even-numbered items). A common theme is given to describe each outcome behaviorally.

A simple Likert-type rating scale is used for each of the outcomes, which are rated from 1 (low) to 10 (high). The 10 outcomes on a 10-point scale provide for 100 total points, which can then be equated to a percentage score. Each team member selects the rating that best describes his or her team on each outcome. The Team Development Rating Scale is presented as Figure 6.1.

The items for the rating scale were selected from a review of group development theory stages (Hare, 1976; Lacoursiere, 1980; Tuckman, 1965) and revised with data from team building models (McGregor, 1960; Shonk, 1982; Woodcock & Francis, 1981) and direct observation of task-oriented groups. Although groups and teams spend most of their time during a particular stage focusing on the outcomes related to that stage, Lacoursiere (1980) provided a graphic description that time is spent at each stage on all of the outcomes.

Kormanski, (1990) reported that the Pearson product moment correlations (Ryan, Joiner, & Ryan, 1985) for each item with the total

TABLE 6.1 *Integration of Group Development Stages and Team Building Outcomes*

Tuckman Stage	Group Development		Team Building		
	Task Behavior	Relationship Behavior	General Theme	Task Outcome	Relationship Outcome
1. Forming	Orientation	Dependency	Awareness	Commitment	Acceptance
2. Storming	Resistance	Hostility	Conflict	Clarification	Belonging
3. Norming	Communication	Cohesion	Cooperation	Involvement	Support
4. Performing	Problem solving	Interdependence	Productivity	Achievement	Pride
5. Adjourning	Termination	Disengagement	Separation	Recognition	Satisfaction

Note: Adapted from C. L. Kormanski & A. Mozenter (1987), "A New Model of Team Building: A Technology for Today and Tomorrow," in J. W. Pfeiffer (Ed.), *The 1987 Annual: Developing Human Resources* (pp. 255–268), San Diego, CA: Pfeiffer & Co. Used with permission.

INSTRUCTIONS: Provide a rating from **one** *(low)* to **ten** *(high)* by circling the appropriate number that you think is most descriptive of your team.

1. **Commitment** — Team members understand group goals and are committed to them.

10	9	8	7	6	5	4	3	2	1

2. **Acceptance** — Team members are friendly, concerned, and interested in each other.

10	9	8	7	6	5	4	3	2	1

3. **Clarification** — Team members acknowledge and confront conflict openly.

10	9	8	7	6	5	4	3	2	1

4. **Belonging** — Team members listen with understanding to others.

10	9	8	7	6	5	4	3	2	1

5. **Involvement** — Team members include others in the decision-making process.

10	9	8	7	6	5	4	3	2	1

6. **Support** — Team members recognize and respect individual differences.

10	9	8	7	6	5	4	3	2	1

7. **Achievement** — Team members contribute ideas and solutions to problems.

10	9	8	7	6	5	4	3	2	1

8. **Pride** — Team members value the contributions and ideas of others.

10	9	8	7	6	5	4	3	2	1

9. **Recognition** — Team members recognize and reward team performance.

10	9	8	7	6	5	4	3	2	1

10. **Satisfaction** — Team members encourage and appreciate comments about team efforts.

10	9	8	7	6	5	4	3	2	1

Note: Reprinted from J. W. Pfeiffer (Ed.), *The 1987 Annual: Developing Human Resources,* (p. 261). Copyright 1987 by Pfeiffer & Co., San Diego, CA. Used with permission.

FIGURE 6.1 *Kormanski/Mozenter Team Development Rating Scale*

score for each of the five rating periods ranged from .649 to .897. Cronbach's alpha (Cronbach, 1951), used to demonstrate internal consistency and reliability, ranged from .922 to .958 over the five rating periods (Kormanski, 1990). A more recent study by Kormanski and Bowers (in review) provides external validity data. They examined teams from a college business statistics class who were conducting a telephone survey for a local chapter of a national charity. Teams of 6–8 members met weekly for 11 weeks and completed the team development rating scale, assessed the number of hours spent on the project per week and recorded the number of successful calls completed. A correlation coefficient of $r = -.50$ was obtained by comparing the final team rating with the total hours spent on the project. This would suggest that teams with higher ratings were more efficient and required less time to complete their task.

Final team ratings were also correlated with the number of successful calls completed. When teams were categorized by score patterns, the following correlation coefficients resulted. The increasing score pattern was $r = .56$, the variable score pattern was $r = .09$ and the decreasing score pattern was $r = -.81$. These correlations suggest that the highest rated teams (increasing score pattern) worked fewer hours and successfully completed the most calls.

▼ TEAM DEVELOPMENT PATTERNS

When all of the components of the preceding chapters of this book are viewed together, a process emerges that has multiple applications in an organizational setting. Some of the applications of this process include the following:

▼ A plan to design team building programs within organizational settings;
▼ A set of realistic expectations concerning team development stages, sequences, and themes;
▼ A basis for setting achievement-motivated goals for team development;
▼ A method of assessing team development progress; and
▼ A diagnostic technique for identifying blockages and suggesting interventions.

The Team Development Rating Scale (Kormanski & Mozenter, 1987) provides data related to the last two points.

For a 10-year period, Kormanski (1990), using the Team Development Rating Scale, collected data from over 50 teams of 5 to 15 members in a variety of different settings for a variety of time frames. These data were always fed back to the team members for their use by a consultant or facilitator as a component of team building training.

Twenty-nine of the teams were composed of undergraduate students enrolled in an academic self-improvement course. The data from five weekly ratings by these groups were used to demonstrate three patterns of team development (Kormanski, 1990): Six teams demonstrated an increasing score pattern (superior teams), 2 teams demonstrated a decreasing pattern (inferior teams), and 21 teams demonstrated a variable pattern (typical teams). Figure 6.2 presents the three patterns. The variable, or typical score, pattern follows the stages of group development. This pattern begins with optimistically high ratings (usually in the 80th percentile) and then shows decreased ratings during the storming stage of conflict. Following conflict resolution, there is a gradual increase to near or above the initial rating. Kormanski noted two subpatterns during the conflict stage. The first involved one rating decrease that was lower than that for the forming stage of the group. The second involved two low points with a slight increase between them. Finally, during the latter stages of typical score pattern and the increasing score pattern, a slight score decrease may occur as a result of resistance to the adjourning process.

The three types of patterns described by these results provide additional information about group and team development (Kormanski, 1990). Some group development stage theories (Hare, 1976; Tuckman, 1965) and team development models (Moosbruker, 1987; Woodcock & Francis, 1981) describe the storming stage of conflict as unproductive for both task and relationship outcomes. The variable score pattern supports these assertions. In addition, an extension of these theories and models would suggest that unmanaged conflict would result in decreased group or team productivity as represented by the decreasing score pattern.

One explanation for the increasing score pattern of the superior teams would be that certain superteams manage conflict in a healthy

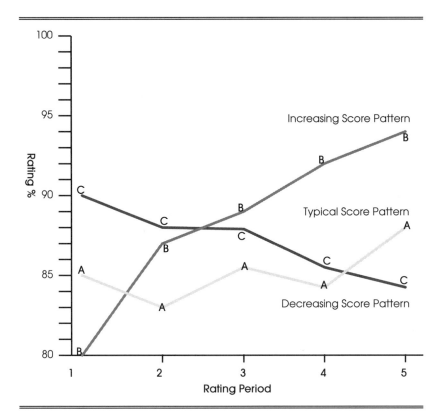

FIGURE 6.2 *Patterns of Team Development*

manner such that task productivity and relationship compatibility do not suffer (Kormanski, 1990). Schutz (1982) suggested that high compatibility and high productivity are related and that increases in interpersonal relations would increase performance. The increasing score pattern supports these hypotheses.

Burns (1978) commented that in small groups more importance is too often given to achieving consensus and minimizing conflict. A study by Hill (1975) with paired teams found that groups with moderate conflict resulted in higher productivity than those with low levels of conflict. These results challenged the team compatibility idea and encouraged some diversity and conflict instead of harmony. Lacoursiere (1980) and Carew et al. (1990) further described this interaction of moderate conflict and productivity by providing separate graphs for task and relationship functions. Both noted that the task function gradually increased while the relationship function decreased during the conflict stage and then increased during subsequent group stages.

The increasing score pattern supports the hypotheses of Schutz (1982) and provides additional support for the development of superior teams Kormanski (1990). Foushee (1984) argued for the same conclusion in his study of factors affecting group process and air crew performance.

The variable score pattern noted by Kormanski (1990) follows the team descriptions of Hill (1975) but differs somewhat from those of Lacoursiere (1980) and Carew et al. (1990) in that ratings for both relationship functions and task functions decreased during the conflict stage. One explanation could be the unstructured nature of the teams studied as Ivancevich (1974) found both the variable and increasing score patterns present in a study of first level managers in a large manufacturing organization. Structured leadership resulted in increasing productivity while unstructured leadership produced a productivity decline at the conflict stage that paralleled the decrease in relationship behavior. Another possible explanation would be that the current research has team members rating task outcomes as opposed to researchers measuring directly an actual performance outcome (Robinson & Robinson, 1995).

The decreasing score pattern reflects descriptions of groups and teams whose development is arrested or who disband due to either too much conflict (chaos) or too little conflict (apathy) (Kormanski, 1990). Zurcher (1969) studied 12 neighborhood action committees using participant observers to assess stage development. Nine of the committees disbanded prior to reaching the final two stages. Although data are not available in the literature, a fourth pattern might be suggested for teams with short life spans. An undifferentiated pattern could occur that would have neither an upward nor a downward trend but would vacillate throughout the life of the team (Kormanski, 1990). The work of Glickman et al. (1987) has suggested this as a distinct possibility.

▼ TEAM LEADER INTERVENTIONS

Teams progress through the stages of group development toward the performance outcomes described by the Team Development Rating Scale (Kormanski & Mozenter, 1987). At each stage, task and relationship challenges are resolved. Leader interventions are called for when teams get fixated at a particular stage, when regression occurs, or to speed up the normal developmental process.

Kormanski (1996a) identified a critical issue at each stage of group development as well as a set of team development interventions for use by team leaders and facilitators. The issues he identified are structure, conflict, supportive helpfulness, team risk taking, and bringing closure. As a team forms, structure is important. However, too much structure leads to a narrow focus, and too little structure encourages a lack of focus. As noted previously, conflict is central to the storming stage. However, too much conflict leads to chaos, and too little conflict promotes apathy. The issue during norming is supportive helpfulness. Team leaders who are too helpful return the team to a dependency state, while those who are unhelpful cause confusion and counterdependency by reducing needed support. During the performing stage, team risk taking is the major challenge. Radical risk taking can result in team disasters, while being too conservative may result in limited accomplishments. Bringing closure is critical during the final stage of adjourning. Attempts to impose additional work on the team as well as failure to attend to unfinished business increase anxiety and make termination difficult.

Team leaders and facilitators must use their knowledge about group dynamics to analyze team situations and diagnose team and member needs in order to make effective and timely interventions. In addition to those interventions that are corrective in nature, the following developmental interventions will aid group progress if delivered at the appropriate group development stage (Kormanski, 1996b).

STAGE 1: FORMING

▼ Allow time for members to get acquainted
▼ Provide essential information about content and process

- ▼ Emphasize new skills required
- ▼ Identify and relate key team values to the current task
- ▼ Share stories of past accomplishments and celebrations
- ▼ Create a team vision of outcome possibilities
- ▼ Set goals to achieve the vision

STAGE 2: STORMING

- ▼ Act assertively and set parameters for the team
- ▼ Listen attentively to all viewpoints
- ▼ Use mediation, negotiation, and arbitration
- ▼ Consider new perspectives and alternatives
- ▼ Suggest and solicit different ways to view the problem

STAGE 3: NORMING

- ▼ Provide opportunity for involvement by all
- ▼ Provide opportunity for members to learn from and assist one another
- ▼ Model and encourage supportive behavior
- ▼ Open communication lines
- ▼ Provide positive and corrective task-related feedback
- ▼ Add some humor and fun to the work setting

STAGE 4: PERFORMING

- ▼ Reward and recognize performance outcomes and positive work relationships
- ▼ Involve the team in group problem solving and visioning
- ▼ Share decision-making opportunities
- ▼ Examine how implementation of team goals will affect the team and the rest of the organization
- ▼ Use delegation to foster professional development

STAGE 5: ADJOURNING

- ▼ Provide evaluative performance feedback
- ▼ Review task and working relationships

▼ Create a celebration activity with emphasis on recognition and fun

▼ Conduct a closure ceremony to signify the project's conclusion

▼ TEAM DEVELOPMENT APPLICATIONS

Alex, Irma, Grace, and Ron had all used the Team Development Rating Scale in the past. They discussed some of the specific applications after talking more generally about team building. Alex had served as a consultant to an expanding restaurant chain. To assist the management team, he collected Team Development Rating Scale data for two new restaurants. The data were used to analyze team development patterns and to assess the impact of a start-up team of experienced managers who were on-site at the restaurants for the first 6 weeks to provide training for the new management teams. Ratings were obtained every 2 weeks for a 6-month period. Figure 6.3 presents the data in graph format.

Both management teams began with ratings in the 50th percentile, and their scores increased rapidly during the first 6 weeks to near or above 80%. This was the increasing score pattern noted in the student study. When the start-up team left, the pattern leveled off, experienced a slight decrease or two, and then showed a slight increase as the scores stabilized in the top 10% of the rating scale. This second phase represented the variable, or typical, pattern.

Irma had consulted with the middle management team of a home for the elderly who were completing the Team Development Rating Scale monthly for a year as part of their training program. Figure 6.4 presents the data for 11 ratings (none were completed during the month of December). The ratings increased rapidly during the active training part of the consultation in the spring. A slight decrease occurred followed by slight increases then slight decreases again, during which time a fall training program began. The increasing pattern returned as a January training intervention was initiated. The overall pattern was variable, with two decreases sandwiched between three increasing patterns.

For his senior thesis, Grace's son, now one of the coordinators of the resident assistant program at his college, analyzed team building

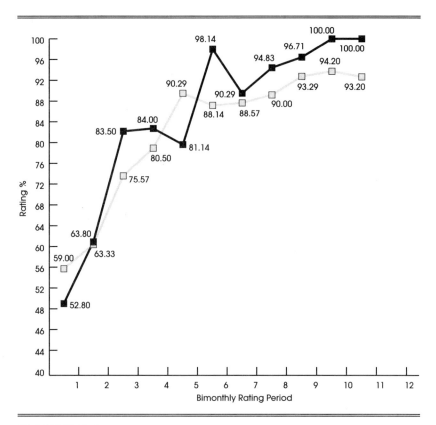

FIGURE 6.3 *Team Development Patterns of New Restaurant Management Teams*

data that his co-coordinator had collected over a 3-year period from resident assistant teams using the Team Development Rating Scale. At each monthly staff meeting, the resident assistants had rated themselves as a team. Grace's son had participated during the previous year but not the first two. Grace had recently read her son's study and noticed how his team followed the normal pattern but the ratings for the teams of the prior two years had gradually worsened over the academic year resulting in a decreasing score pattern.

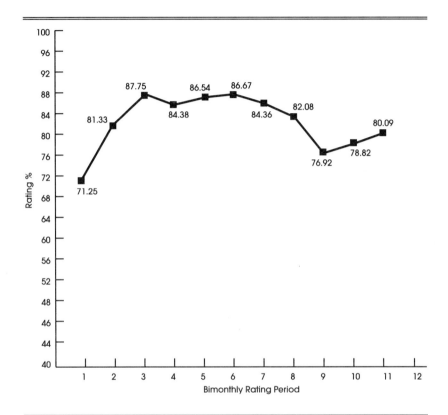

FIGURE 6.4 *Team Development Pattern of a Home for the Elderly Management Team*

Grace's son noted that the coordinator for each of the first two teams had served in that position for only that particular year but that he had been in that position for 2 years. Even though the relationship between team leadership and team performance is a complex one, the data suggest that effective leadership may have a positive influence on team development. The study demonstrated that the typical team performance is significantly different from that of inferior teams, which show decreasing score patterns when rated by team members. Figure 6.5 presents a graph of the results of the 3-year study.

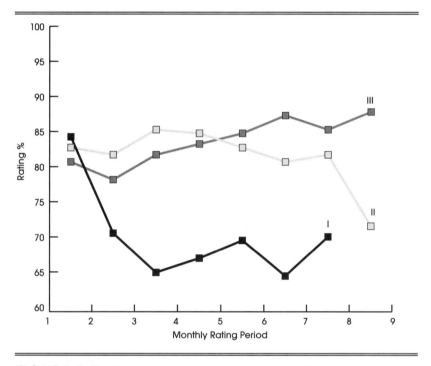

FIGURE 6.5 *Team Development Patterns of Resident Assistant Teams*

During the fall semester, the women's volleyball coach at Ron's university had talked with Ron about some strategies for increasing team cohesion. They shared with one another their knowledge and experiences concerning teams and team leadership. The coach had a strong, veteran returning team and wanted to maintain the high morale and high performance that were present in the preseason practice.

Ron met with the team and shared his understanding of group development sequences and team development patterns. All agreed to complete the Team Development Rating Scale (Kormanski & Mozenter, 1987) every 2 weeks throughout the season. Ron agreed to analyze the results and provide feedback at team meetings. The team then set goals for the upcoming season.

The veteran team quickly achieved commitment and acceptance. Competition for the few remaining starting positions highlighted the conflict stage. Once team roles were established and standards clarified, the coach indicated that everyone would get adequate playing time if goal progress was maintained. An early close game solidified the team and fostered a sense of belonging.

The coach talked with Ron during the cooperation (norming) stage concerning performance lapses following player errors. Interestingly, it was not the player making the mistake but her teammates who felt badly, which, in turn, affected their performance. To increase team involvement and support, a strategy was devised at the next team meeting to have the veteran players monitor mistakes and increase their involvement and supportive behaviors to *all* team members following performance miscues.

At the beginning of the productivity (performing) stage and near the end of the season, the team suffered their two regular-season losses. Because the losses occurred immediately before team meetings and team development ratings, Ron anticipated lowered ratings. The ratings remained high, however, as a result of the coach's leadership style, which reinforced the players' growing vision of themselves as a championship team. The result was a harder working, more determined group of young women. Achievement and pride highlighted end-of-season wins.

The play-offs began the termination stage, and the team approached these significant events with a high cohesive, high concentration level. As a result of their skill and teamwork, they received two championship trophies, one for each league in which they participated. Both satisfaction and recognition outcomes were reached. Throughout the season team ratings had remained high. Figure 6.6 presents the team development ratings for this superior team.

Irma commented that teams were increasing everywhere, not just in business and education. Alex added, "Those of us who have been trained as counselors can engage in a lot more roles than just provide counseling for individuals." Grace recalled that one of their initial discussions focused on group process and the reemerging roles of process observer, process facilitator, and process consultant. Ron suggested that

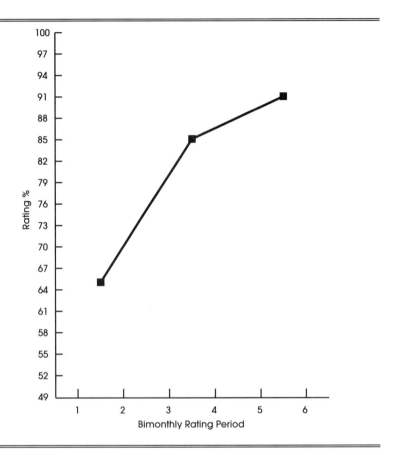

FIGURE 6.6 *Team Development Pattern of a Superior Women's Volleyball Team*

training team leaders and facilitators was another possibility for those with excellent expertise and understanding of group dynamics and team development.

As their meeting drew to a close, the team talked at length about what their next discussion topic should be. Ron finally suggested that since team membership could involve a substantial amount of diversity, team member diversity might be the next focus for the team.

Choosing their specific topics was more difficult than ever for every member of the team. Each was convinced that diversity was the most challenging topic they had chosen thus far and the most critical one to understand.

"The more diversity you have, the more perspectives you will get," Irma said. "However," noted Grace, "if you have too many viewpoints, the early stages of team development will require more time." "And more expert leadership will be needed as well," added Ron. Alex concurred, noting that the conflict would probably be more complex and that controlling change would demand all the knowledge and skills they had been discussing.

The team struggled with selecting their individual topics and discussed whether they should continue to mail their summaries to the other members prior to their meetings. As the meeting concluded, none of the four were able to choose a specific topic, but all agreed to write something about diversity. "In the past, presenting ideas in written form has helped our discussions," stated Grace. The others agreed. Alex then contributed the fact that the team format provided them with an opportunity to apply their ideas immediately, and Irma felt the team format had resulted in a much more open and exciting learning experience. Ron mentioned that their writings and discussions had already provided enough material to send to an editor for publication considerations but that the diversity component was essential to the manuscript if it was to address relevant and critical issues. The discussion wound down, and arrangements were made for the next meeting.

Team Member Diversity

I have a dream today.
—Martin Luther King, Jr.

When Grace, Ron, Irma, and Alex met for their first meeting of the new year, Grace began the discussion by admitting to really having struggled to record something about her topic. "My value system," she told the others, "has always supported diversity issues, but my knowledge and experiences have been very limited. My choice was a personal one. I decided to write about social identity development. Most of my colleagues are unaware that I have a learning disability, and it's not something I share easily. It has made my academic life quite a challenge, as I have never sought out assistance or special treatment but basically acquired some knowledge about this condition and applied it to myself.

"I have always had difficulty with written symbols and the written language in general. My biggest problems are with handwriting, syntax, and spelling. Since I have never been able to write everything I've wanted to say, I've found other means to express myself. Drama helped me increase my interpersonal skills, and art became a favorite pastime. Computer and secretarial help have allowed me to contribute to our current project, but I was extremely apprehensive when Ron first suggested that we write material for our subsequent meetings. Without a doubt, my learning disability has helped to shape my social identity. Therefore, that is the topic which I chose."

Ron noted a parallel thinking process for his topic selection. "My color as an African-American has always forced diversity upon me," he noted. "I have attempted to balance my quest for my own black identity with an understanding of the backgrounds and cultures of others. Spending most of my work life in academic settings has kept me protected at times, but every now and then, I get a reality jolt from some unexpected part of society. The rational part of me keeps saying I have the potential to link multiple cultures together because of where I have been and who I am. But, I do have some uncertainty about how effective I can be. For that reason, I decided to research racial-ethnic identity development for this meeting."

Irma was amazed that everyone, she included, was contributing a personal example. "Is it because of our development as a team," she wondered aloud, "or because of how we grew as individuals, or both?" She told the others that she had always had a strong commitment to gender as a diversity issue. "It started when I developed anorexia as a teenager," she commented. "Conquering that condition brought me a new awareness of the gender expectations that our society imposes on both women and men. That's probably why I volunteer to run so many support groups in my free time. Researching gender identity development seemed a natural outgrowth of my interests."

Alex spoke next. He began by apologizing for not mailing the others his summary and confessed that he had actually left his writing on the topic at home. "My plan was to plead being too busy at work and with the holiday season. However, I did write something. My topic was personal, too, and it involved a struggle. My experiences have been powerful, but I have rarely shared them, not even with close professional colleagues or family. I became fully aware that I was gay during my last year of college. I had indications before that, of course, but I always quickly covered them up by actively choosing and engaging in extreme opposite alternatives. Since college, I have tried not to stay in any one job for a long time period, have been careful in selecting my friends, and have literally stayed in the closet with my sexual orientation. Being part of this team and pursuing our goals together has given me a new sense of identity and purpose in life, and I feel I can now disclose my constant struggle with all of you. For this meeting I did research on sexual identity development."

The team continued their discussion quietly but enthusiastically focusing upon their reactions to the recent self-disclosures. Each offered helpful feedback without being evaluative. The dialogue that evolved was more of a celebration of diversity. The team then discussed their research in more detail, and Alex agreed to mail the others his writing on diversity. Their summaries follow.

▼ SOCIAL IDENTITY DEVELOPMENT

Identity development has both an individual and a social nature. Individual development theories such as those of Erickson (1968), Loevinger (1976), and Chickering (1969) are popular with counselors, psychologists, and educators. Also useful for understanding individual behavior are more specific developmental theories that involve thinking (Piaget, 1970), moral values (Kohlberg, 1981), and careers (Holland, 1973).

Social development involves relationships with people, groups, teams, and communities. As our social mobility continues to increase, so does the diversity of our personal contacts. This expanding diversity can be represented by a full range of differences, including age, gender, race, ethnicity, culture, geography, and religion, as well as differences in specific skills, personalities, and experiences.

Halverson and Cue'llar (1996) described three stages of social identity development as a basis for understanding the diversity issues of team development. During an initial stage of dependence, which occurs during the forming of the team, both dominant status members and subordinate status members accept the standards set by the dominant group and ignore issues of diversity. During the second stage, counterdependence, there is an awareness of differences in privileges and feelings of oppression. When confronted by this new awareness, members of the dominant status group often feel guilt and an inability to be genuine with members of the subordinate status group. They may continue to ignore the differences, overcompensate or attempt to be realistic and authentic. Subordinate status members usually are reactive and express external anger about their treatment in the previous dependent stage. They often feel internal anger concerning what each has given up. These behaviors, attitudes, and feelings provide the fuel for the storming stage, when the group members interact with their different perspectives regarding content issues and the tasks of the team.

The third stage, independence, is characterized by a coming together to work against the oppressive outcomes of the previous counterdependence stage. Members form and expand rational and authentic relationships. Common ground is identified, and issues of disagreement are temporarily set aside to be addressed at a later time. This norming process encourages open dialogue about issues of diversity and about the readiness level of each team member.

Bennis and Shepard (1956) were the first to suggest a group development theory that followed the pattern Halverson and Cue'llar later described. Bennis and Shepard used the name "resolution" for the independence stage and included a fourth stage, "interdependence," which represented the productive working of the group or team. At this fourth level, team members would independently increase their understanding of their own social and cultural identity while also being dependent on the other members for sharing and integrating their diversity with the team.

Halverson and Cue'llar (1996) used an awareness of racism and sexism to build their model of social identity, but they have since generalized the model to other types of social diversity. They named the developmental stages of teams infancy (dependent), adolescence (counterdependent), and adulthood (independent). Because their model was created to address the formation of interdependent work teams, a fourth stage, representing this goal, could logically be named seniorhood!

Griggs and Louw (1995) used the Tuckman (1965) model to discuss diversity in high performance work teams. They described the forming stage as beginning with members initiating their relationships with one another. The initial relationships are typically calm and tentative, with discomfort residing beneath the surface. Members become aware of subtle yet serious differences, and attention is usually given to the more irrelevant differences. Team leaders can best intervene by using skills that uncover the relevant issues. Interventions should address sources of discomfort, examine the overall vision of the team, and differentiate between cultural misunderstandings, diversity issues, and relationship dynamics. An appropriate goal is to identify and expand members' common ground about differences.

During the storming stage there is a focus upon the surfacing conflict. Relevant differences along with suppressed emotions begin to surface. Cycles of hostility appear. Team members move to extreme positions and become highly ethnocentric. Expressions of handling conflict differ across cultures and need to be handled differently for different cultures, which raises concerns regarding equality. Understanding the meaning and intention behind the expression is a major challenge. Team leaders should select interventions that build, bridge, and develop understanding. A key skill is to listen with cultural understanding. The use of self-disclosure, accurate empathy, and genuineness can help clarify communication messages. Leaders should admit mistakes openly and not avoid conflict situations. The goal is to facilitate process development and interpersonal relationships, and to do that the leader must help group members understand their differences.

During the norming stage, the team is forged. As team members wrestle with differences and similarities, their overall comfort level begins to increase. The team members explore ways to work together, and the team starts to build its own culture and value set. Cohesion occurs as the communication process becomes more effective. The team leader may now use interventions that draw attention to balance. It is important for the team leader to increase the use of feedback throughout the team, to create opportunities for individuals to contribute their talents, and to identify and clarify ambiguities. An appropriate goal is to help the team members recognize and respect individual differences.

The performing stage involves leveraging differences. Team members assume increased responsibility for team tasks and coopera-tiveness in all relationships. The common vision drives the team and reflects the organizational mission and values. A self-correcting cycle is in place, which confronts appropriate conflicts, implements action plans, and promotes a synergistic working relationship. Team leaders are now able to utilize interventions that combine differences and sim-ilarities. Creative tension is accepted as a means of achieving higher team performance levels. Continued and constant opportunities for learning are valued. Both relationship building and task effectiveness are viewed as critical processes that can always be improved. Team approaches are chosen over individual approaches. An appropriate goal is to assist the team members in integrating and using their individual differences for the common good of the team.

During the adjourning stage, although not addressed by Griggs and Louw (1995), team members would recognize and celebrate both individual differences and their unity as a team.

The value of organizational diversity is promoted by the achieve-ment of team performance outcomes and the teamwork that contributed to those accomplishments. Halverson and Cue'llar (1996) identified five specific benefits that can result from the use of multicultural teams. These include the following:

▼ increased creativity and different perspectives;

▼ decreased tendency toward conformity;

▼ insights resulting from previous exclusions of minority members;

▼ challenges to examine current procedures and norms; and

▼ use of cultural strengths of all team members.

The social identity development of a team thus presents a new set of complex challenges for the team leader and team members. Meeting those challenges requires a comprehensive understanding of both individual development across cultures and the cultural norms of the developing group within an organization.

▼ RACIAL-ETHNIC IDENTITY DEVELOPMENT

Professional practitioners frequently use Cross's (1971) identity development model to gain a better understanding of the developmental pattern for people of different cultures in their groups. The five-stage model has a thematic and sequential pattern that is similar to the pattern in group development theories when viewed from a broad perspective.

The initial preencounter stage involves the rejection of one's own cultural group and assimilation into the majority culture. In the team setting, this would occur during the forming stage. The desire for assimilation suggests a willing team member, while the rejection of one's own culture indicates a team member who is inexperienced. Increased awareness as a result of orientation to the tasks of the group and reduced dependency on the leadership open the door for conflict.

Conflict is a vital component of the next two stages of identity development. In the team setting, the storming process encourages unwilling and inexperienced team members to behave in counterdependent ways. The encounter, or second, stage of identity development is characterized by dissonance and confusion and is followed by a third stage of immersion-emersion, which involves resistance and then rejection of the dominant culture.

The fourth stage, internalization, involves a reconciliation of personal autonomy. This norming process provides the team members with relevant experiences although they often are still unwilling or unconfident. Increased communication and cohesion encourage reaching out to others of both the minority and majority culture.

The final stage of internalization-commitment results in a meaningful understanding of the new self and one's important place in the minority community. The willing, experienced team member embraces the performing process, which offers action opportunities that contribute to the task accomplishment and builds the solid relationships of the team.

The five stages of the Cross (1971) identity model parallel the first four stages of Tuckman's (1965) group development model. There are two stages of conflict but no adjourning stage, which Tuckman and Jensen (1977) added later. A helpful descriptive analysis of a minority culture individual moving through the five stages of identity development is provided in Brinson (1996).

The changing nature of the workforce along with its increasing diversity will require greater understanding of racial-ethnic cultures. Team leaders can maximize the effect of their teams by using interventions that provide growth opportunities for identity development as well as group development. The new global marketplace will respond more positively to multicultural strategies devised by a team of diverse members who are culturally sensitive.

Brinson (1996) suggested that reflecting on the following series of questions will increase one's potential for continued development of cultural sensitivity when working with individuals from different cultures:

▼ Think training. How were you trained as a professional? Has your training continued?

▼ Think identity development. How comfortable are you when working with others? What else do you need to know?

▼ Think world view. How strong are your beliefs and values? How do they compare with others'?

▼ Think friendships. How selective are you in making friends? What criteria do you use?

▼ Think ethnicity. How appreciative are you of differences? What intimidates you?

▼ Think "ideal" American. Does everyone have an equal chance for success? What restricts access and opportunity?

▼ Think political divisiveness. How influenced are you by the media and public opinion? On what issues will you take a stand?

▼ Think professional involvement. Are your actions congruent with your attitudes and values? Are you a good role model?

▼ Think cultural awareness. What stereotypes still persist in society? How often do you discover yourself using them?

▼ Think acquiring knowledge. How do you learn best? What evidence do you have of recent learning?

Chavez (1994) challenged the assumptions that individuals within majority and minority cultures are radically different and that there will be overwhelming resistance in the workplace to the inclusion of minority cultures. She suggested that accommodating different cultures (race or ethnicity) in the workplace is not the major problem. Instead, the problem rests with education and the poor preparation of many segments of our population for the contemporary workforce. Because many of the groups receiving a poor education are from minority cultures, there is frequently a focus on the need to increase cultural awareness while improvements to the educational system are neglected.

▼ GENDER IDENTITY DEVELOPMENT

Helms (1990) presented a model of female identity development that parallels Cross's (1971) theory and consists of four stages named after the first four stages in Cross's work. The four stages are preencounter, encounter, immersion-emersion, and internalization. Progress through the stages represents a movement from passivity to active involvement in influencing one's personal development. As with the Cross model, there is a relationship between the stages of the Helms model and those of the Tuckman model of group development.

Tuckman's first two stages of forming and storming match Helms's preencounter and encounter stages. In Helms's model, the first stage involves a passive acceptance of a traditional sex role as a key determinant of the forming process, and the second stage begins the storming process of questioning and exploring alternative viewpoints. The immersion-emersion stage has two phases. The first phase, characterized by an active rejection of a male-controlled society, is a continuation of the Tuckman storming stage. The second phase represents a movement into the Tuckman norming stage as women seek out positive role models and relationships with other females. Finally, the internalization stage involves active involvement in the performing process of living one's standards and values. As with other identity development models, little attention is given to the adjourning process (Tuckman & Jensen, 1977).

Downing and Roush (1985) also provided a model of feminist identity that parallels Cross's theory. Their five-stage sequence includes passive acceptance, revelation, embeddedness-emanation, synthesis, and active commitment. O'Neil and Roberts Carroll (1988) described a gender role journey in similar terms using the five phases of acceptance, ambivalence, anger, activism, and integration-celebration.

In the Downing and Roush model, the initial stage of passive acceptance places women in a traditional and stereotypical role. Teams are frequently formed in traditional ways by traditional organizations and outdated systems. Men are viewed as superior and assume key leadership roles. Female team members, like male team members, begin the forming stage as willing but inexperienced participants. The state of initial dependency is often prolonged as both genders collude to avoid the natural transition to the storming stage. Thus, when the transition occurs, feelings of anger, guilt, and related emotions accompany its onset.

The revelation stage, which parallels Tuckman's storming stage, is usually brought about by a series of crises with strong counterdependent undertones and the aforementioned emotional content. A dualistic thinking pattern challenges obvious inequities and the willingness of the team members disappears. A major task for team leaders of both genders is to provide unwilling, inexperienced team members of both genders with opportunities for clarification and understanding as well as to support their participation and involvement in the team.

The storming process continues in the embeddedness-emanation stage as women affirm and strengthen their new identity through networking and connecting with selected role models and colleagues. In the team setting, experimenting with new behaviors and establishing cautious interactions with men provide a resolution to the resistance and hostility as well as a transition to the establishment of meaningful norms.

During the synthesis stage women draw on these relevant experiences as well as their cautious interactions with men to begin the development of an authentic and positive feminist identity. Experienced but unconfident team members still require support and encouragement, but they also need participative involvement at a responsible level. This norming process allows women to transcend typical sex roles and evaluate men on an individual basis.

The active commitment stage is a performing one. Willing, experienced women function as true team members and take part in shared leadership roles. The feminist identity is consolidated and the team is viewed as a nonsexist world in which men are considered equal but different. Meaningful, interdependent working relationships are now possible.

Downing and Roush's five stages of identity development are similar to those described by Helms (1990) and Cross (1971) and relate to the task and relationship dimensions of the Tuckman model (1965). Each of these identity development models includes two stages that fit within Tuckman's conflict stage, and none include the final adjourning stage postulated by Tuckman and Jensen (1977).

Carter and Parks (1996) demonstrated that the attitudes and mental health of black and white women reveal different patterns, thus suggesting that attention must be given to within-group differences as well as to overall gender identity characteristics. They also made the point that there is room in Helms's model for traditional women with highly developed identities.

Models also exist for male development. Horne, Jollif, and Roth (1996) offered a model of male development when they described five developmental influences on men. According to Horne et al., nurturing, role modeling, initiation, mentoring, and eldering occur in a sequential order and, as shown in the following paragraph, correspond fairly well to the five stages of the Tuckman and Jensen model (1977).

The forming stage of male development provides the first influential interaction as male parental bonding expands the nurturing relationship from the mother to the father. As the male child's gender identity develops, his self-concept is formed, with the relationship to the father being a primary resource. During the storming stage, the male adolescent moves beyond the parental relationship and encounters a variety of role modeling experiences that foster aspirations and help to build ideals. These experiences may include challenges and related learning opportunities.

The norming stage involves the initiation into manhood, and this rite of passage is celebrated in a variety of symbolic ways. The American culture has not provided for this initiation as well as other cultures and often allows it to be done by the peer group, which fails miserably (Horne et al., 1996).

During the performing stage the developmental process continues with meaningful mentoring relationships. The man shifts his focus to a broader perspective of the world around him. He becomes more egalitarian and nurturing and less competitive and self-centered. He experiences an increase in self-awareness and reflection. He is genuinely concerned about the next generation.

The adjourning stage involves eldering and the new role of sage. The man's senior status provides him with opportunities for giving away acquisitions through his generosity and knowledge through his wisdom. This role, too, has not been encouraged by the American culture, and frequently our potential sages are consumed by financial burdens and degenerative diseases (Horne et al., 1996).

A challenge for the leaders of teams and groups that are task focused is to provide direction and support to both the group as a unit and individuals within the unit based on their respective readiness levels. In addition to performing this transactional leadership role, leaders are encouraged to provide the transformational interaction that inspires and influences both the personal and professional growth of the individual and the unit.

▼ SEXUAL IDENTITY DEVELOPMENT

Cass's (1984) sexual identity formation model is a comprehensive presentation of homosexual development that is backed by strong empirical research. In the model, a prestage is followed by six formal stages—confusion, comparison, tolerance, acceptance, pride, and synthesis—in a developmental sequence.

The prestage is a forming phase in which individuals follow a heterosexual lifestyle without question even though subtle signs suggest a different sexual orientation. Their willing but inexperienced behavior builds the tension that initiates the six formal stages that follow.

The storming process characterizes both the confusion and comparison stages. Unwilling, inexperienced individuals know homosexuality has something to do with the uncertainty they feel but fail to see direct connections. Then as the insights begin to appear, they make comparisons and become somewhat sure, but not quite certain, of the homosexuality pattern. Feelings of being different and being very much alone are common.

By the tolerance stage, the individuals have enough experience to know that they are homosexual but are unconfident. As the norming process begins to provide some support, they still interact with heterosexuals but find themselves attracted to homosexuals. They often hide their homosexuality because they think it may be temporary and may go away over time. The future is very scary for them.

The norming process continues into the acceptance stage, when the certainty of their homosexuality is confirmed. Now, they will inform a few selected people, but only in confidence. They are not confrontative and want only to be part of a work or social setting. They do, however, increase the time they spend interacting with homosexuals.

The first phase of the performing process signifies the beginning of the pride stage, as willing, experienced individuals begin to feel proud about their homosexual lifestyle. They wear symbolic objects declaring their sexual orientation, talk openly about their lifestyle, and become angry when they see acts of discrimination against homosexuals. The synthesis stage completes the performing process. The individuals now feel more confident and comfortable about their sexual orientation. They will tell anyone about themselves. Their anger is more controlled and less impulsive. They value relationships with both heterosexuals and homosexuals.

Homosexuality can have additional interactive complexity when other diversity characteristics, such as age, gender, race, ethnicity, disability and health, are a part of the total mix. For example, because of the misinformed view that AIDS is a gay disease, homosexuals are frequently categorized as deviant, sick, and immoral (Corey & Corey, 1993). As with other minority groups, homosexuals are confronted with an abundance of stereotypes, prejudices, and misconceptions about their behavior and its cause.

In the team setting, a member who is a gay or lesbian may develop strong feelings of cohesion and trust with the group as the team moves through its own developmental process. These feelings may encourage the individual to make public his or her sexual orientation. Positive reactions may not always follow this revelation, and the team may be forced to tackle an additional crisis as the group development sequence regresses toward the storming stage. The gay or lesbian individual may experience the same regression and begin to feel very alone and very different.

Clark (1987) provided some helpful guidelines for those who want to support gay and lesbian individuals:

▼ Suspend judgmental thoughts.
▼ Ascertain if support is wanted or needed.
▼ Treat interactions and information confidentially.
▼ Encourage personal growth and development.
▼ Seek congruence with yourself before aiding others.

The next step would be to offer help and support in the same manner one might use when confronting any type of discrimination or abuse.

▼ COMPARING MODELS

As Irma, Ron, Grace, and Alex discussed their research, they noted that they had each used the Tuckman model of group development as a comparison point, and they recalled that in their writings on team building they had each used the Kormanski and Mozenter model of team development. They worked together to create Table 7.1, which presents

TABLE 7.1 *A Comparison of Group, Team, and Social Identity Development Models*

Model	Stage 1	2	3	4
Group Development				
Bennis & Shepard (1956)	Dependence	Counter-dependence	Independence	Interdependence
Tuckman (1965)	Forming	Storming	Norming	Performing
Team Development				
Kormanski & Mozenter (1987)	Awareness	Conflict	Cooperation	Productivity
Griggs & Louw (1995)	Initiating the relationship	Surfacing conflict	Forging a team	Leveraging differences
Halverson & Cue'llar (1996)	Infancy	Adolescence	Adulthood	(Seniorhood)
Social Identity Development				
Cross (1971)	Preencounter	Encounter, Immersion-Emersion	Internalization	Internalization-Commitment
Cass (1984)	Prestage	Confusion, Comparison	Tolerance, Acceptance	Pride, Synthesis
Helms (1990)	Preencounter	Encounter, Immersion-Emersion (rejection phase)	Immersion-Emersion (Support Phase)	Internalization
Horne, Jolliff, & Roth (1996)	Nurturing	Role modeling	Initiating	Mentoring

a comparison of group, team, and social identity development models. Irma pointed out that the models have a high degree of similarity when behavioral descriptions are examined and that terminology often accounts for the biggest difference. Ron suggested that Irma's insight was helpful in viewing the big picture of models and theories. Alex noted, however, that there can be subtle differences when models are translated into behaviors and that effective leaders must be flexible and willing to change behaviors quickly when the need becomes apparent. Grace agreed and emphasized the need to use common sense and take into account situational variables when making decisions.

Irma noted how Ron and she were focusing on the theoretical and global perspective, whereas Alex and Grace were concerned with the more specific details and factual data. Having just conducted a personality exploration workshop with couples, she wondered if the differences and similarities of their personalities had added to the interactive dynamics of their team. Grace told the others that she had taken the Myers-Briggs Type Indicator (MBTI) recently and had learned a lot about herself. Ron noted that he often used the MBTI with classes to match personalities and occupational interests. Alex added that he had taken the MBTI as part of a seminar on improving interpersonal relations in the workplace. Irma, who had begun the discussion and had given the MBTI to her recent workshop participants, suggested that they might want to talk about their personalities and temperament types at their next meeting. They were all certain that each had a very different personality type and that these differences represented another dimension of diversity.

▼ DISCUSSION OF PERSONALITIES

When the team met for their second meeting of the new year and their discussion of personalities, all brought data from their experiences with the Myers-Briggs Type Indicator. Grace pointed out that the MBTI was, as its name suggests, an indicator, not a test, and that it provided descriptive, not evaluative, data. She further added that the MBTI was one of the most frequently used assessment instruments in the United States.

Irma noted that the MBTI is meant to identify preferences when you have a choice; thus, it is about how you would like to function, not how you actually do function. She suggested that many people filling out the MBTI do not understand this and consider their frequency of behavior, not preferences, when answering the questions posed.

Ron noted that based on his experience, about one-fourth of those who take the MBTI receive a score that may not reflect their actual preferences. He emphasized the need for trained counselors and facilitators to provide clarification when scores are given to those who have taken the inventory, since the score is only one piece of the data. He suggested that, when possible, workshop exercises, readings, discussions, and additional follow-up activities be used to confirm each preference and a specific personality type. He concluded by noting that the MBTI was, in his view, one of the most abused instruments in the marketplace.

Alex told the others about a criterion he used for assessing type validity. He noted that when one is in his or her preference, it is energy sustaining, and when one is in a nonpreference, it is energy draining. Furthermore, when a person is in a preference, he or she feels more comfortable, more confident, and more competent. But he noted that these are only feelings and stressed that the MBTI does not measure or identify abilities.

All agreed that no questions or theory can fully explain the complexity of the human personality and that the MBTI does not and should not be used to categorize people, but only to help understand them. They continued to emphasize that the MBTI attempts to measure only four sets of preferences, namely, two attitudes regarding energy source and energy direction and two behaviors concerning individual perception and judgment. Grace had brought two handouts, one of which summarized the personality preferences and another that summarized a common grouping called personality temperaments. They are presented in the next two sections.

▼ MYERS-BRIGGS PREFERENCES

The work of Isabelle Briggs Myers (1980) provides depth to the understanding of personalities. The Myers-Briggs typologies she created with her mother, Katherine Briggs, were originally used in personality research but their use soon spread to career development and counseling, to religious formation and spirituality, to teaching and learning styles, and eventually to the business community. Team building, work relationships, and leadership can all profit from the use of the instrument in a variety of settings.

Based on the theories of Carl Jung (1971), the Myers-Briggs Type Indicator reports a person's preference on four scales (Myers, 1993). Each scale represents a dichotomy between two attitudes or two behaviors. The initial attitudinal dichotomy identifies the source of one's energy, with some individuals preferring the outer world of people and activities (**E**xtroverts) and others the inner world (**I**ntroverts) of ideas and reflections. The two behavioral dichotomies describe how individuals solve problems. Thus, the second preference involves perception and how information is acquired. Some people prefer to use their senses and factual reality (**S**ensors) while others prefer inspiration and possibilities (i**N**tuition). The third preference focuses upon how individuals make judgments and reach conclusions. Some people consider logic and make decisions objectively (**T**hinkers) while others consider people and make decisions subjectively (**F**eelers). A final attitudinal dichotomy describes one's preference for a lifestyle in the outer world and emphasizes the use of one of the two behaviors. Some people use more thinking or feeling and prefer to make decisions quickly to achieve closure (**J**udgers) while others prefer to keep options open and continue to collect data by sensing or intuition (**P**erceivers). Thus, each individual has a natural preference for one of each of four opposites, although each individual uses all eight. The four sets of preferred choices (E/I; S/N; T/F; J/P) result in 16 personality types (Myers, 1980).

▼ PERSONALITY TEMPERAMENTS

Keirsey and Bates (1984) categorized the 16 Myers-Briggs typologies into four temperaments. Their grouping is not based on the typology theories of Myers and Jung but upon the widest possible base of accurate behavioral predictions (Kroeger & Thruesen, 1988). The four temperaments are the guardians (SJ), the artisans (SP), the idealists (NF), and the rationals (NT).

Guardians (SJ) are traditionalists. They seek to belong to meaningful organizations. They are precise, take-charge leaders who hold subordinates accountable. For them, authority is the system. As team members, they are superdependable, loyal, and functional. They focus on organized procedures and abhor disorganization.

Artisans (SP) are negotiators. They strive for action. They are practical, problem-solving leaders who are quick starters and resourceful. For them, authority is the moment. As team members, they are adaptable, flexible, and spontaneous. They implement tasks in a clever, immediate way. They dislike routine and hierarchies.

Idealists (NF) are catalysts. They are in a constant search for identity. They are high relationship leaders who put people first. For them, authority is the person. As team members, they are cooperative, supportive, and empathetic. They think about possibilities for people and dislike the guilt feelings they have when they cannot do enough.

Rationals (NT) are visionaries. They work to improve their competence. As leaders, they are architects of change, theoretical, and independent. For them, authority is competence. As team members, they are intellectually curious, high achievers, and complex. They design systems that promote learning and are frustrated by incompetence.

Keirsey and Bates (1984) suggested that effectiveness can be enhanced by pairing individuals who have the potential to complement one another. Teamwork that requires equal attention to tasks and relationships might be accomplished by a guardian (SJ) and an idealist (NF). Tasks that require an equal amount of planning and implementation may profit from a rational (NT) and an artisan (SP).

▼ DISCUSSION OF TEMPERAMENTS AND TYPES

Irma initiated the sharing of temperament and type by recalling a discussion the team had concerning learning styles during their second meeting. Each had described a different preference for learning. "So we probably have different temperaments and, thus, personality types," she noted. Irma then described herself as having an idealist temperament (NF). She pointed out her constant search for authenticity and meaning in life, as well as her involvement with and concern for people. She also described herself as a warm, enthusiastic planner of change who is imaginative, individualistic, and impulsive. As an ENFP type, she said that she seeks to understand and inspire others.

Alex saw himself as an artisan (SP) who has a hunger for freedom and a willingness to take risks. He provided a picture of himself as a realistic adapter in an environment of material things who is easy going and tolerant as well as a sensible, practical observer of details. As an ESTP, he said that he enjoys hands-on experiences and a challenging crisis.

Grace revealed that she was a guardian (SJ) who worked diligently to bring order and stability to her life and the organizations with which she was involved. She viewed herself as a sympathetic organizer of facts and details who is concerned with the welfare of others as well as prizing service and productivity. As an ISTJ, she said that she understands the need to conserve and protect our institutional values.

Ron presented himself as a rational (NT) who is intrigued and challenged by conceptual abstractions. He described himself as a logical, decisive innovator of ideas whose favorite competitor is himself. As an INTJ, he said that he is seriously intent on designing complex systems to enhance learning and foster developmental change.

Irma continued her leadership role by suggesting that they might form pairs to work on their next writing assignment. Ron noted that since rationals and artisans complement one another, Alex and he could work together to explore the topic of leadership style and personality. Grace added that Irma and she, an idealist and a guardian, might work together on the complementary topic of team membership and personality.

The pairs mailed their summaries to one another before their next meeting, which was held in March. At the meeting they all expressed how pleased they were with how well they had worked with their partners. Their research summaries are presented next.

▼ LEADERSHIP AND PERSONALITY

Fiedler (1967) was one of the first to identify personality as an important contributor to leadership. His studies of least preferred coworkers (LPCs) demonstrated that some leaders have a preference for task behaviors and others for relationship behaviors. In addition, he found that high task-oriented leaders work best in highly structured or highly unstructured situations whereas relationship-oriented leaders work best in situations that are moderately structured. Finally, the amount of power possessed by the leader was also important in his contingency theory of leadership.

Hersey and Blanchard (1982) continued the work of Fiedler in the development of their Situational Leadership theory. They added another personality descriptor, task maturity level, to match leadership style to a given task. They later changed this variable to readiness level (Hersey, 1984) or developmental level (Blanchard, 1984) and assessed it in terms of a follower's ability and willingness to do a task.

Situational Leadership requires each leader to develop competence with all four styles of leadership—directing, coaching, supporting, and delegating (Hersey & Blanchard, 1982). However, the Myers-Briggs theory notes that each leader has a natural style that is a preference. Furthermore, the relationship between Keirsey temperament types and Situational Leadership styles suggests that, for leaders, specific personality types may be advantageous when working with followers of a given readiness level (Good, Hill, & Blanchard, 1992). Based on descriptive data of a qualitative nature, the following match between the four temperaments and the four leadership styles (S)/readiness (R)/developmental (D) levels is proposed.

As leaders, guardians (SJ) prize belonging and work to build a predictable routine and a stable system. They are superdependable and establish formal and professional working relationships. They are high task and low relationship type leaders. They work best with willing and inexperienced followers (R1,D1) using the telling/directing style (S1).

The artisans (SP) prize action and can deal with concrete problems in a pragmatic fashion. They are at their best in crisis situations and are patient, flexible, and adaptable. These individuals are high task and high relationship type leaders. They have the potential to lead unwilling and inexperienced followers (R2,D2) using selling/coaching style (S2).

The idealists (NF) prize identity and use communication and caring as springboards to building meaningful work relationships. They are enthusiastic and focus on possibilities for people. They are low task and high relationship leaders. They work well with unconfident (or unwilling) and experienced followers (R3,D3) using a participating/supporting style (S3).

The rationals (NT) prize competence and work as architects of change and progress. They are interested in relationships within the organizational system and between other systems. They are low task and low relationship type leaders. They work most effectively with willing and experienced followers (R4,D4) using a delegating style (S4).

Good et al. (1992) presented another variation, suggesting that rationals (NT) are better matched with unwilling, inexperienced (R2,D2) team members and that artisans (SP) work best with willing, experienced (R4,D4) team members. Their position that the rationals (NT) deliver a coaching/selling leadership style (S2) and the artisans provide a delegating leadership style (S4) is based on a face validity study of over 2,000 managers.

A comparison of leader temperament strengths with team member needs at the R2,D2 and R4,D4 levels would encourage questioning of the match proposed by Good et al.. Unwilling, inexperienced followers (R2,D2) would appear to have difficulty with a rational leader (NT) who stresses competence and complexity. In the same manner, experienced, willing followers (R4,D4) might have difficulty with an artisan leader (SP) who focused upon immediate action and risk taking.

A major goal of developing leadership competence is to gain flexibility across the four leadership styles. Thus, the development of all eight Myers-Briggs personality preferences is in order. A leader's biggest mistake is ignoring the importance of balance (Kiser, Humphries, & Bell, 1990). One strategy to achieve the goal of flexibility is to balance a logical, analytical approach to a situation with a personal approach that provides individual consideration and offers inspiration. Barr and Barr (1989) suggested that the most successful leaders have become adept at using both their four personality preferences and their four nonpreferences.

The most effective leaders can combine all four sets of temperament behaviors with the appropriate leadership style for the followers' readiness level. Since the Myers-Briggs preferences do not indicate competence, individuals can develop their nonpreferences as well. Doing so, however, requires additional focus and energy. Experience may also be critical, as Jung (1971) has suggested that midlife is a doorway to developing the nonpreferences.

▼ TEAM MEMBERSHIP AND PERSONALITY

In addition to increasing team effectiveness by matching the appropriate leadership style with follower readiness levels and encouraging shared leadership roles, the team leader can enhance performance possibilities by encouraging team members to take responsibilities based on their personality type and the stage of group or team development. As noted in previous chapters, the stages of group and team development are forming/awareness, storming/conflict, norming/cooperation, performing/productivity, and adjourning/separation.

Myers (1980) stressed the role of the individual's dominant behavior in guiding the personality much like a captain guides a ship. Gaining an awareness of the dominant process and personality type of team members can, when matched with the team building/group development stage, help the team leader determine an effective intervention strategy.

Lawrence (1982) provided brief descriptions of the Myers-Briggs personality types focusing on the dominant mental process as a key variable. He combined two types with the same dominant process to create eight descriptions: organizers (ENTJ/ESTJ); analyzers (INTP/ISTP); adapters (ESTP/ESFP); managers of facts and details (ISTJ/ISFJ); helpers (ISFP/INFP); harmonizers (ESFJ/ENFJ); innovators (INFJ/INTJ); and planners of change (ENFP/ENTP).

During the forming/awareness stage of a team, members with dominant thinking behaviors can be most helpful. Both organizers and analyzers are useful in getting the team oriented and resolving dependency issues, moving the team toward commitment and acceptance. Members with dominant sensing behaviors can make contributions during the storming/conflict stage of a team. Adapters and managers of facts and details are willing to deal with resistance and hostility, which assists in clarification and in moving the team toward greater belonging. At the norming/cooperation stage of a team, members with dominant feeling behaviors have great value. Both helpers and harmonizers can aid in increasing communication and building cohesion to promote involvement and support. Members with dominant intuitive behaviors can be helpful during the performing/productivity stage of a team. Innovators and planners of change are resourceful in solving problems and promoting interdependence, helping team members gain a sense of achievement and pride. During the final stage of adjourning/separation the team's readiness level regresses, and the leadership style, personality temperament, and team member descriptions used during the norming cooperation stage are appropriate. Table 7.2 presents the relationship between group development stage, follower readiness level, leadership style, leader temperament style, and team member types.

Finally, a reminder is in order regarding psychological type and the Myers-Briggs classification system. The four temperaments proposed by Keirsey and Bates (1984) and the 16 Myers-Briggs personality types represent just two of many ways to group individuals based on attitudes and behaviors. Only four variables—two attitudinal and two behavioral—are used. Thus, any type of temperament contains variability within as well as without. As an individual in a workshop noted, even though we may all have the same zip code, we each have different street addresses. Personality types and temperaments can be useful if viewed from a broad perspective for developing managerial planning and implementation strategies and for helping individuals recognize their unique strengths and abilities. As Jung (1971) summarized "Classification does not explain the individual psyche. Nevertheless, an understanding of psychological types opens the way to a better understanding of human psychology in general" (p. 516).

TABLE 7.2 *Relationship Between Group and Team Development Stage, Readiness Level, Leadership Style, Temperament Style, and Team Member Types*

Group and Team Development Stage	Team Readiness Level	Leadership Style	Leader Temperament Style	Team Member Types
1. Forming/Awareness	Inexperienced and willing (R1,D1)	Directing/Telling (S1) (high task and low relationship)	Guardian (SJ)	Organizer & Analyzer (ENTJ, ESTJ & INTP, ISTP)
2. Storming/Conflict	Inexperienced and unwilling (R2,D2)	Coaching/Selling(S2) (high task and high relationship)	Artisan (SP)	Adapter & Manager of Facts & Details (ESTP, ESFP & ISTJ, ISFJ)
3. Norming/ Cooperation	Experienced and unwilling or unconfident (R3,D3)	Supporting/ Participating (S3) (low task and low relationship)	Idealist (NF)	Helper & Harmonizer (ISFP, INFP & ESFJ, ENFJ)
4. Performing/ Productivity	Experienced and willing (R4,D4)	Delegating (S4) (low task and low relationship)	Rational (NT)	Innovator & Planner (INFJ, INTJ & ENFP, ENTP)
5. Adjourning/ Separation	Experienced and unwilling (R3,D3)	Supporting/ Participating (S3) (low task and high relationship)	Idealist (NF)	Helper & Harmonizer (ISFP, INFP & ESFJ, ENFJ)

Note: Adapted from C. L. Kormanski (1996b), "Team Interventions: Moving the Team Forward," in J. W. Pfeiffer (Ed.), *The 1996 Annual: Volume 2, Consulting* (pp. 85–88), San Francisco: Pfeiffer & Co.; and G. Lawrence (1982), *People Types and Tiger Stripes*, Gainesville, FL: Center for Applications of Psychological Type.

Team
Performance

*The true test of the professional is
not what he knows how to do, but
how he behaves when he does not
know what to do.*

—William Oncken, Jr.

*I*n April, Ron, Irma, Alex, and Grace met to examine their progress and look for gaps in their study of teams. Ron wanted to know what was missing in their collection of writings. Irma suggested that they look more closely at what people in teams actually do. Alex agreed, noting that additional applications and examples would be helpful. Grace proposed using case studies from their own experiences to highlight the integration of the theories, models, and principles presented in their writings. Irma said that she had served on the executive board of a state counseling organization for the past 2 years. Grace contributed that she had participated in the strategic planning process of her school district. Alex spoke about his involvement in a countywide community leadership program the previous year that was conducted by the local chamber of commerce. Ron added that he had recently facilitated a continuous quality improvement (CQI) team on his campus. All appeared to be relevant topics for case study presentations.

Once again, a clear direction was agreed upon and a cohesive effort was begun as each team member talked about how best to organize data for inclusion in the case studies. A meeting date and time were established for later that month. As always, the team members mailed their reports to one another prior to the next meeting.

▼ A STATE COUNSELING ASSOCIATION EXECUTIVE BOARD TEAM

Irma was currently beginning her third year on the state counseling association's executive board. In that position, she had recently chaired the planning committee for the highly successful state conference. When she had first joined the board, the leadership was provided by a trio that included the current president, the immediate past president, and the president-elect. The work year for the board began each July with a summer strategic planning workshop facilitated by a former executive board member. At the workshop new members were oriented to the team effort that drove the strategic planning process. The board met six times during the year, often in conjunction with a state conference, workshop, or special event. During the meetings, leadership responsibilities were shared among the entire team, and new members quickly became seasoned veterans. The challenging tasks, limited resources, finite amount of time, large geographical area, and small size of the executive board necessitated rapid involvement and commitment by all. These constraints also created and fueled many of the critical issues the board members faced as they attempted to build a viable association in a rapidly changing environment. Leadership development and leadership succession were major concerns.

As Irma reflected back over the past few years, she realized that the forming stage of group development and the team outcomes of commitment and acceptance were ongoing challenges for the executive board team. Integrating new members into the process while seeking to replace the leadership and experience that left with the departing members was paramount.

During her first year on the board, the strategic issues targeted for attention were organizational development, member recruitment, and legislative action. The executive board team divided into three task forces, one focused on each of the strategic issues, with the president, past president, and president-elect providing the initial leadership to get the team members started on each issue. Everyone agreed that a shared team leadership format was desirable following the formation period. Each task force was charged with the responsibilities of environmental scanning to note recent changes that might impact the organization; identifying informational needs and creating a procedure to access those needs; developing an action plan that would include strategies for acquiring needed resources; and promoting issue accomplishments throughout the association and beyond.

Environmental scanning by the organizational development task force examined political, economic, societal, and technological trends. Key findings were that the current bylaws were out of date; that the association was losing members and financial resources; that the association did not present a consistent professional image to the public; and that rapid technological change was requiring older members of the association to compete with newly trained graduates for a dwindling number of job openings as current positions were collapsed and few new ones were created.

Informational needs acquisition centered on building networks and access to resources for problem solving. Initial ideas for beginning these tasks included creating a leadership mentoring program, identifying opportunities for membership involvement, clarifying roles and responsibilities, developing fund-raising projects, and organizing a public relations effort.

Specific action plans were developed to provide for a sustained leadership transition and training program to be held annually; to establish business partnerships for cooperative ventures and additional funding; to review and revise the mission, bylaws, and vision of the organization; and to increase the size of the task forces by seeking interested individuals from the total membership.

The member recruitment task force found similar trends from their environmental scanning. The association continued to lose members, which resulted in less dues monies, reduced conference attendance, and difficulties in obtaining volunteers to carry out organizational work. Few members were interested in serving on committees, and when people were willing to run for the elected leadership positions there was usually only one candidate for each office. Less monies required the limiting of membership services, which started the cycle all over again by resulting in a reduced membership.

Informational needs that surfaced centered on costs for services. Key questions were the following:

▼ What are the essential services?
▼ Can current dues be lowered?
▼ For what services will members pay?
▼ Can we increase our nondues revenues?
▼ Are unified dues an answer?

The action planning phase resulted in expanding the newsletter; examining the dues structure especially for graduate students; developing a dialogue with the staff of counselor education programs; issuing a membership directory; creating a training and speaker service; and considering the publication of a new journal. (One had been published previously but was discontinued a few years ago.)

Environmental scanning by the legislative action task force re-vealed that the association's legislative action committee and its state licensure committee were duplicating one another's efforts. The task force also found that theirs was one of the few states that did not have a counselor licensure law.

Informational needs identified by the legislative action task force involved understanding the state legislation process, seeking support from other human services organizations within the state, and obtain-ing assistance from the national counseling association and states that had achieved licensure.

Action planning began by combining the association's legislative and licensure committees. In addition, plans were formed for legisla-tive task force members to take part in a national government relations training program, to update a list of professionals who would actively support the process of licensure including the necessary fund-raising, and to cooperate with the other task forces to increase association membership.

By the end of Irma's first year on the executive board team, the association's networking process had improved; counselor educator involvement had increased; and graduate students were taking more active roles in the association. In addition, the newsletter had been expanded and now appeared on time; conference attendance had increased; a state licensure effort had begun again; emerging leaders had been added to the executive board; and the strategic planning process continued to provide a futuristic direction.

The next year, change and growth continued. The organizational development task force became the task force on organizational struc-ture and gave special attention to leadership development, membership roles, and financial resources. The membership recruitment task force reduced its focus to membership services and sought to improve the newsletter, conferences, and workshops, the association's advocacy role, and public relations. It also continued exploring the possibility of a journal. A new professionalization task force focused on the state licensure effort and legislative action. It also began to promote ethics, standards, research, and scholarship. Finally, a visioning task force was developed that addressed the continuity of the strategic planning process, the association's historical roots and heritage, and its organizational vitality.

As Irma completed her second year on the board, she was pleased with her involvement as the state conference chair and with her contributions to the membership services task force. She reflected on how the forming process was renewed each summer as new members joined the executive board team. The subsequent storming and norming continued the process of shaping the issues and the resulting action plans for the performing stage. At the end of the academic year, the team adjourned and a new team met the next year.

As Irma's third year began, the strategic issues were going through another change. Only the membership services and visioning task forces remained. As strategic issues became operational and the organization gained control over them and was able to manage them with its normal allotment of resources, strategic attention shifted to emerging new issues and significant aspects of strategic issues that were still unresolved. Service to the community was a new emerging issue; funding sources and public awareness were continued concerns of past strategic issues.

Thus, a core of ongoing issues was typically handled by an officer or a committee that had been assigned that responsibility. Special task forces and resources were mobilized to address issues that were directly related to the survival of the association.

At a recent executive board meeting, Irma, now a seasoned veteran, was asked to provide some feedback to the team. She identified the annual forming of the new team as the most critical event for the association. Furthermore, she pointed out that providing structure was an essential leadership intervention early in the life of the team. She noted that extremes in structure were usually dangerous: Too little structure created delays and ambiguities concerning the task; too much structure resulted in a narrow task focus and discouraged different viewpoints and perspectives. She encouraged the use of a high task, low relationship leadership style at the forming stage to provide a balanced structure that would ensure a positive beginning for the team. As the meeting came to a close, Irma felt pleased with her contributions to the team and her concern for the team members. She felt that her choice to become involved with this association had been a good one.

▼ A SCHOOL DISTRICT STRATEGIC PLANNING TEAM

When Grace's school district began strategic planning 3 years ago as a result of a state mandate, Grace immediately joined the planning team, as she felt her unique perspective of student development was needed for this important work. The team consisted of a broad representation of concerned individuals from throughout the school district, which was located in a rural part of the state. Team member selection was accomplished by inviting specific individuals based upon their school and community roles and issuing an open invitation to anyone in the school district who wished to participate. Approximately 25 individuals volunteered and served as the initial core group. The team included students, teachers, parents, administrators, school staff (counselor, nurse, etc.), school board members, community representatives, and the superintendent. The team leader was the director of curriculum, who had previously been the high school principal. A consultant from a local university served as the team facilitator. The team was now finishing its third year, and one third of the membership had changed.

The first year had been an exciting and emotional experience for all involved. The state mandate not only required that each school district have in place a formal strategic planning process but also specified task deadlines for reporting progress. In addition, it required that a new outcomes based education (OBE) model that was still controversial in the state be adopted. The state did not provide much structure or assistance in the implementation of the process, but it did allow for a decent amount of freedom and flexibility.

The team leader and facilitator built a sound structure that welcomed all who volunteered but also engaged everyone in the "hard work" of planning during a period of imposed change. The objective of the team throughout the strategic planning process was to maintain the positive aspects of the existing curriculum and integrate the new outcomes based education components over a 2-year period. The intent was to incorporate the OBE components, not eliminate or replace the existing structure. A complementary goal was to increase standards in order to prepare more competent graduates.

Following an orientation and introduction to the strategic planning process, each work session began with the team participating in small training modules. At the work sessions, the team examined the history of the school district, conducted a needs analysis, prioritized critical issues, surveyed the demographics, and began to develop action plans.

Task forces were used to conduct the needs analysis, prepare the demographic survey, and develop a mission statement based on core values. Midway through this process, the team began to develop a vision statement. Specific groups were also asked to collect data on current practices involving professional development and assessment. The major effort, however, was the revision of the curriculum. Content area task forces were formed, and half-day and evening work sessions were scheduled to address nine broad content areas. In addition to the task force members, representatives from all stakeholders were invited to the sessions as were local experts for the content areas. The nine areas were communication, mathematics, science/technology, environment, citizenship, the arts, careers, wellness, and home economics. The content task forces identified desired outcomes, specific goals, and a detailed implementation plan. Teacher in-service programs added to this developmental process by contributing instructional and assessment strategies.

The strategic planning team prepared a two volume compilation of the data generated by the task forces. Specific changes and innovations the strategic planning team proposed included more stringent graduation requirements than mandated by the state, portfolio assessments, a major high school project for each graduate, a teacher induction program, a diversity statement, and a comprehensive revision of the entire curriculum.

As the first year ended, the statements of mission and vision had been refined and validated. Both are reprinted here.

MISSION STATEMENT

As the leader in an educational partnership with the community, it is the mission of the school district to ensure that all students discover and develop their talents and abilities, acquire respect for self and others, and obtain the knowledge and skills to succeed and contribute to their highest potential as ethical, responsible citizens in a rapidly changing global society through a challenging, comprehensive program taught by an exceptional staff in a secure, caring environment.

VISION STATEMENT

The vision of the school district is to establish and maintain an alliance among students, parents, community, administrators, teachers and staff, which will continually adapt to new situations by improving the education offered to our students in order to prepare them for the ever-changing challenges of life.

The team's comprehensive plan was adopted by the school board and approved by the state's department of education. A dinner celebration was held to reward all the participants and the strategic planning team members received "I survived strategic planning" T-shirts designed by one of the student members.

In Grace's view, the storming stage of group development with its outcomes of clarification and belonging was the most challenging time frame for the strategic planning team. Fueled by the statewide controversy over outcomes based education, this mandated change process involved a group of individuals with initial mind-sets that were extremely defensive and resistant to change. Emotions ran high, and unfounded gossip and rumors provided opportunities for constant fire-fighting. The energy level, however, was high, and the initial objective of improving the curriculum, not dismantling it, offered the team members a challenge when "preparing our graduates for the future" was agreed upon as a driving force. The "hard work" of the meetings quickly screened out those who would not "walk the talk" as well as single issue volunteers.

The following school year, the newly elected state governor indicated that he would soon abolish the outcomes based education model. Most of the state's school districts stopped their strategic planning process and decided to wait to see what would happen next. The strategic planning team in Grace's school district, with the support of the school board and the superintendent (who were represented on the team), chose to continue the process and shape their own future. The team's planning had gone far beyond the state requirements, and the team members really felt they had ownership of an important role in the school district. The team had accomplished the essential outcome of the strategic planning process, which is not to just develop a plan but to create strategic planners, and continued its hard work. The team's mission, values, and vision were firmly established and used to revise the curriculum and general organization of the school district.

As the team's third year began, Grace noticed that team members were beginning to leave and that, periodically, replacements were added to maintain the stakeholder representation. About one third of the original group remained, providing the necessary shared leadership to continue. Some loose ends were completed early in the year, and a few additional issues were targeted. Each new issue attracted some additional interested individuals, and the changing team composition required a recycling through the forming, storming, and norming stages. Some resource people were also brought onboard as a result of special needs.

As the school year progressed, team meetings occurred more sporadically and the strategic planning process slowed down, as did the team members' emotions associated with the current issues. By spring, the energy level of the team changed. Concerns about the school district's discipline policy had increased and communications to the school board, the administration, and the superintendent about issues of fairness, equality, and common sense had begun to multiply. Following a discussion with his administrative staff, the superintendent quickly brought the issue to the strategic planning team. The rationale of the superintendent for this action made sense. The issue was emotionally charged, was increasing in frequency, needed input from all the stakeholders in the district, and required a complex set of solutions that would address both the present and the future.

The strategic planning team mobilized quickly around the new issue which the superintendent hoped to have resolved by the end of the next school year. As the forming stage began, the team defined the issue and described a vision of the ideal discipline policy. Next, they sought viewpoints from a variety of stakeholders and discovered that school bus drivers were not represented. By the next team meeting, three bus drivers had joined the group. The storming stage moved smoothly with healthy conflict as the team members worked to establish a policy that would be fair and equal for all grade levels. Everyone rallied around a key criterion that stated that the discipline process should be an educational experience. The team completed a rough draft of the discipline policy by the end of the summer and a final draft by fall. School board approval and school district implementation occurred before winter began.

Following the holiday vacation period, the team met and prioritized issues for the remaining months of the school year. Four task forces were created. One group was assigned to revisit the curriculum and assess its relevancy. A second group would collect data on the changing demographics of the school district. The third group would examine the current physical plant and related facilities and project future building needs. The fourth group would conduct a gap analysis of the current strategic plan and determine what would be necessary to bring the plan up to date.

In a conversation with the team leader, Grace was asked her perception of what made the team so successful over an extended period of time. She pointed out that the team had been given a major challenge each year and had chosen a pathway that led into healthy conflict and created within the team a clarification of the task and a sense of belonging. She felt that the storming stage brought out the best in the team. In addition, the core group of team members modeled a strong work ethic and put the education of students at the center of their work. Plus, the team avoided the extremes of too much conflict, which creates chaos, and too little conflict, which encourages apathy. Grace concluded on a personal note. She commented that she had usually stifled conflict in the past but that this team had encouraged her to participate in a different manner, which had resulted in a much more satisfying learning experience.

▼ A COMMUNITY LEADERSHIP TEAM

Alex had been selected by his company to participate in a leadership development program conducted by the local chamber of commerce.

The rationale for the program was to encourage individuals to become more active in their community by seeking elected office, serving on organizational boards, accepting leadership roles, and participating as volunteers. One-day workshops were held once a month from fall through spring. Each workshop heightened awareness and built skills related to a critical topic or current need. The class that was formed worked together throughout the year, beginning with an introductory weekend retreat, continuing on through the completion of a class project, and ending with a visionary graduation program. The potential for networking among a variety of people was an added incentive for all the participants.

For Alex, both the program and the participants contributed to a number of insightful experiences. The leadership was provided by the chamber's executive director, a professional facilitator, and a steering committee of community leaders representing a broad spectrum of talent and experiences. All took an active part in the promotion, selection, design, implementation, and evaluation of the program.

A welcoming reception provided a brief get-acquainted opportunity and an orientation to the program. The weekend retreat, conducted by two professional consultants, established the program's purpose of community involvement and building a supportive network by creating a shared vision for the future of the county. Alex enjoyed the experiential learning activities and small group discussions at the retreat. He found that designing a symbolic vision that addressed the issues facing the community was a challenging but rewarding, enjoyable, and meaningful task. The forming process of the team was moving full-steam ahead.

The first workshop explored the culture and heritage of the area and the second examined economic development. Workshops on government and health care followed. The fifth workshop focused on leadership and team development and like the weekend retreat included a strong experiential array of group exercises plus a revisit to the vision. The next three workshops focused on education, housing, and human services. The final workshop involved the integration of the total program learning outcomes into the ongoing vision. The evening of that session was a celebrative affair, with a visionary scenario being presented by the program participants to an audience of spouses, friends, community business leaders, participants of past programs, and steering team members. Alex found the experience exhilarating and was extremely proud of the work done by the team and the close relationships that were formed.

With regard to group process, the storming stage became very apparent during the fourth workshop when the participants began a discussion of the class project. A number of ideas were proposed, but none received majority support. The consensus that teamwork is supposed to produce did not materialize. The conflict escalated. As they did for each component of each workshop, the participants rated the class project discussion for its meaningfulness, usefulness, and contributions to leadership development in the county. The rating for discussion was 68%, which proved to be one of the four lowest ratings of all the workshop components for the entire program.

At the fifth workshop, the class project discussion continued with additional ideas being suggested. The conflict continued but never became chaotic. The energy level remained high, and everyone participated. The rating for the second class project discussion was 77%, which was still a fairly low rating. The class agreed to continue the discussion by meeting between sessions. A strong effort was made to include everyone by scheduling meetings at a variety of times and places. Specific consideration was given for people with disabilities to accommodate one of the class members.

The norming stage began to appear as a project was selected. Cohesion among the team members increased and communication channels opened as everyone engaged in the project planning process. The class reached consensus; their project would be to add to the program's orientation reception. They planned to turn this September event into a fund-raising dinner and to invite previous classes to welcome the new class. Committees were formed for marketing, finance, site selection/catering, and special events. At the eighth workshop, the component rating for the third class project discussion remained at 77%, but the committees continued their high productivity levels.

The final workshop brought the efforts of the four committee's together. Everyone was included in the decision making, and those with individual differences were major contributors. The component rating for the fourth class project discussion was 93%, the third highest rating of all components for the entire program. The big event was scheduled for mid-September at a local amusement park. The dinner was to be informal and held outdoors.

The event was a huge success. The turnout was excellent, a large amount of money was raised for program scholarships, and everyone had fun. Alex had been asked to speak to the new class as part of their orientation. He talked briefly about the stages of group development, singling out norming as the most critical stage for his class. Once major differences were resolved, coordination of the planning effort was essential. Individuals who had promoted the idea that was eventually selected assumed the early leadership. However, they were willing to share this critical role, and others stepped forward as needed. Everyone found a way to contribute. Alex told the new class that helpfulness was a key intervention strategy. Team members whose initial ideas were not selected might have easily been unhelpful and resistant. The other extreme could also have slowed down progress, as some overhelpful people often do everything themselves, excluding those who sincerely want to contribute in meaningful ways. He concluded that shared leadership, open communication, helpfulness in task accomplishment, and the cohesive building of supportive relationships were all essential to the success of the class project.

Following the class project event, Alex decided to volunteer with a few community organizations that might benefit from his experiences. He also planned to talk with his boss about sponsoring a scholarship for someone with a diversity background to participate in a future leadership class. Alex was glad he had made the decision to participate. It had not been an easy decision, and he had considered dropping out during the fall. Taking part in the class project was the magnet that kept him involved. He saw the entire project as a real crisis and an opportunity for his particular leadership style and expertise to make a difference. As a result of his commitment to the project, he discovered some important qualities that he possessed that were needed right now in the community.

▼ A UNIVERSITY CONTINUOUS QUALITY IMPROVEMENT TEAM

Ron had been asked by the continuous quality improvement steering team at his university to cofacilitate a CQI team involving the maintenance staff. The task would be challenging because of a number of unique variables. First, it would involve unionized employees. Second, they all worked the third shift from 11 P.M. to 7 A.M. Meetings of the team would, therefore, be at 11 P.M. A faculty member from the business department agreed to be the other cofacilitator. A training program was offered, and the entire shift participated. From that group, five individuals volunteered to be on the team.

The two facilitators met with the supervisor of the physical plant, the sponsor of the team, to establish parameters and specify the mandates under which the team would operate. The sponsor agreed to allow the team to elect its leader and choose the process for improvement. The team leader, the process, or both, could have been selected by the sponsor. These decisions were not preordained and were situational in nature. Thus, each decision was unique. The sponsor did set two mandates: (1) Assigned work for the shift must be accomplished and meet or exceed standards; and (2) all involved must abide by the union contract.

The team gathered for their first meeting in mid-July and elected a team leader. He would be responsible for making the meetings' arrangements, starting and finishing the meetings on time, communicating information and participating in each sign-off procedure with the cofacilitators and the sponsor. The model the team chose to use involved a seven-step sequence:

1. Defining the process for improvement.
2. Describing the process.
3. Measuring the process.
4. Identifying root causes.
5. Developing solutions.
6. Implementing solutions.
7. Evaluating improvements.

Upon completion of each step, the team leader and cofacilitators would meet with the sponsor to assess the team's progress and agree on direction. A formal sign-off procedure was used to ensure that this agreement occurred throughout the process and to enhance understanding of the rationale for each action taken.

As its focus, the team chose to improve the process of ordering and distributing cleaning supplies for their shift and called themselves the supply distribution team. During the next month and a half, they clarified the process currently in use, conducted a needs analysis, interviewed users, and identified a variety of issues related to the process. By early September, the process was defined and an issue statement was agreed upon by all. The first sign-off was accomplished and the following issue statement was accepted: "Improve distribution of supplies by using uniform products to adequately stock work areas where regularly scheduled ordering is followed by timely deliveries." This statement addressed the major needs of users, appeared achievable in a reasonable amount of time, and contained performance elements that were measurable.

Two months later, in early December, a flow chart of the current process was developed and accepted, and sign-off two was completed. The complexity of what was thought to be a simple process was astounding to the team members. Bottlenecks and subsequent wait states were everywhere. Ordering forms were complicated; there was no accurate inventory because supplies were scattered throughout the warehouse; many different products were used for the same job; ordering was done randomly and based upon the foreman's available time; deliveries were unpredictable; and the entire process lacked structure, causing it to be ineffective and inefficient. The team began to realize that they could not only improve the effectiveness and efficiency of the process, thus making everyone's job easier, but they could also probably save the university some money.

Before the year ended, the team had identified some indicators for measuring the current process. Called critical success indicators (CSIs), the team would use these to demonstrate change when the task was completed. The average wait gap between the department's receival of ordering forms and its delivery of supplies was one CSI. The initial process performance chart developed by the team revealed that, for the current process, this time period averaged 4 days with a range of 2 to 8 days. The percent of order the department delivered, was also calculated but was found to be consistently around 97% and was discontinued as a critical success indicator after a brief monitoring period. Another indicator the team measured was the length of the ordering form, which was five pages long and contained 144 items.

By February of the new year, the team had analyzed fish-bone diagrams to assess cause and effect relationships. From that analysis, they identified 11 root causes of ineffectiveness and inefficiency in the process and subdivided them into three categories: factors under the control of the maintenance department, factors under the control of the university, and factors that were uncontrollable. The four root-cause factors under the control of the maintenance department were:

▼ The ordering of supplies was complicated.
▼ Computer inventorying was not current or accurate.
▼ Delivering supplies was time consuming.
▼ Personnel vacation time and special events added additional work.

The two root-cause factors under control of the university were:

▼ Nonmaintenance items were stored in the warehouse.
▼ External suppliers were unpredictable.

The five root-cause factors that were uncontrollable were:

▼ Resources were limited.
▼ Cleaning buildings requires adequate supplies.
▼ Emergency tasks take priority ahead of supply delivery.
▼ The consequences for not cleaning buildings were unpleasant.
▼ Such factors as weather and personnel illnesses were unpredictable.

As the team completed sign-off four, it became apparent that all of the bottlenecks on the flow chart were related directly or indirectly to the root causes they had identified.

Sign-off five was achieved in early March as the team established a list of musts and wants. Included as "must" criteria were abiding by sponsor mandates, scheduled deliveries, timely deliveries, and solution monitoring and feedback. Listed as "wants" were reduced paperwork, a warehouse assessment, and an accurate inventory of cleaning supplies. The team considered the musts essential and the wants highly desirable in solution development. Finally they determined that all of the solutions should contribute to eliminating critical causes, meeting customer needs, timely implementation, and improving the process of supply distribution.

Using these criteria along with the data they had previously generated, the team selected the following six solutions for implementation:

1. Revise the delivery system
   a. Obtain feedback from experienced workers
   b. Develop a schedule for deliveries
   c. Use second shift to make deliveries
2. Increase the use of uniform products
3. Simplify order form
4. Organize the warehouse
5. Reorganize the janitors' closets
6. Improve the accuracy of the computer inventory

A two-by-two matrix check sheet was completed to ensure that all six solutions met the musts and wants criteria.

The team spent the rest of the spring developing an implementation plan. The plan included checkpoints for team and sponsor review; updated the process performance measures (the wait gap between receiving order forms and supply delivery); and stated what actions would be taken by whom and when.

Within a year, the supply distribution team had formed, stormed, and normed. The team had organized, resolved conflicts, and established performance standards. During that time period, the foreman of the shift was replaced, vacation schedules disrupted the team's progress, one team member was transferred, one left the team, and one died of cancer. Thus, a number of relationship concerns were intertwined with the team's task concerns.

Step six involved implementing the planned solutions. Everyone thought this step could be accomplished by fall. However, barriers seemed to appear out of nowhere, and progress slowed to a snail's pace. Some of the proposed changes required approval from higher officials; a storage facility the team had considered critical to the warehousing of supplies was needed for another purpose (a temporary auxiliary classroom); computer problems complicated the inventory changes; and the team's product standardization effort was held up by one of the suppliers. By September, the team had completed only 3 of the 11 tasks they had delineated for implementing the six solutions. A few more tasks were partially completed during the next 5 months.

Ron and his cofacilitator struggled with their role. They looked for ways to be positive but always remained persistent. The team now consisted of only two members, a team leader, and the two cofacilitators. No one gave up, however, and the team completed small tasks to augment the overall plan while remaining in a holding pattern on some of the larger tasks. Then, in February, everything seemed to happen at once, with each event making it easier for the team to implement the next sequential task.

Early the previous fall, personnel from the second shift had begun delivering supplies when they emptied waste receptacles, a regular schedule of ordering and delivering supplies was established, and the janitorial closets were reorganized. The order form was eventually reduced from five pages to one and some benchmarking regarding warehouse organization was done. In February, the warehouse was reorganized; (liquid) Solution Centers for standard cleaning products were installed; and computerization of the inventory process moved forward dramatically. All at once, everything fell into place.

The team completed sign-off six in mid-March; this step had taken 9 months. Step seven and the subsequent sign-off was completed by the end of March as four critical results were accomplished:

1. Uniform Products: Only 10 regular, standard cleaning products were now being used, and all were stocked at 13 Solution Centers. Overall costs were reduced by the use of standard products.

2. Well Stocked Warehouse: All products were now located in one warehouse row. Two- to 3-weeks of stock were kept on hand. All janitorial closets were now secure with appropriate locks.
3. Regular Ordering: The order form was reduced from five pages to one page. A once-a-month ordering process had been implemented.
4. Timely Deliveries: Delivery time was reduced from an average of 4 days to 2 or fewer days. The second shift was now making the deliveries. A new key system had been installed for access to janitorial closets and the warehouse.

Everyone throughout the organization was pleased with the results. A celebration breakfast (the team's shift ended at 7 A.M.) was held, and the team received watches. Throughout the ensuing year, their efforts were recognized in a variety of university publications and events.

Ron and his cofacilitator wrote one of the articles. They noted that the performing stage had been the most critical for this team. The interdependent relationships among the team members and their persistence in problem solving were strong contributors to the outcomes of achievement and pride. Furthermore, the improvements that resulted directly affected their, and their colleagues', work efforts. Often, teams set unrealistic goals that are too high or unchallenging ones that are too low. The former have no emotional penalty, as no one really expects the team to accomplish them, and the latter, though relatively safe, may not result in any significant improvements. By using moderate risk-taking in developing goals that were challenging *and* realistic, this team had been able to develop and implement their solutions. Ron had always enjoyed competitive, personal challenges, but he was particularly elated about being a part of a highly successful team effort. This had been a new experience for him.

▼ ADJOURNING THE TEAM

Irma noted that their own team was really a fifth case study. "We have been together for a significant amount of time, built strong relationships, and are almost finished with our writing task," she said. "Our forming period was spent orienting ourselves to the task and resolving dependency issues. We explored group development theories and gathered data about groups and teams. Agreeing on a balanced structure was the key to moving us forward."

Grace suggested that their attention to change and conflict moved them into the storming period. "We struggled with our emotions and differences of opinion, got a little edgy with one another, and became somewhat frustrated with ourselves. The resistance was there, as was some under-the-surface hostility. Our understanding of healthy conflict as a normally occurring event and a prerequisite to change was insightful. Of course, accepting change as a given and choosing to influence it was the attitude that moved us forward to the next stage."

Alex reflected on the norming period. "We integrated a lot of theories, models, and experiences into our presentations on task groups, leadership style, and team building. As a working team, we also established our own standards and guidelines. There was a lot of shared leadership, joint decision making, and mutual support. We did regress to the storming stage every now and then, but we remained there for only a brief stay, which proves we really did learn something. My personal esteem, which was quite low at the beginning, increased dramatically during this time. Participative helpfulness was critical to our progress at this juncture."

Ron assumed the leadership next by commenting that their decision to tackle team member diversity and share personal applications provided the impetus for the team to reach the performing period. "Our interdependence became strong with our self-disclosures as we listened to and supported one another. Our problem-solving capabilities were apparent in each of the case studies and in our ability to learn from our own team experiences. Moderate risk taking by each of us was the essential ingredient at this stage. No one took the safe route, although we all considered it, nor did anyone gamble with extreme risk taking. Both the self-disclosures and the feedback were timely, specific, and relevant."

Grace introduced the topic for their next meeting, though all had been thinking about it, by pointing out that the adjourning stage was next for the team. "This stage usually creates a crisis," noted Alex. Irma added that the more successful the team, the bigger the crisis would likely be. Ron suggested that they should use what they had learned and increase their relationship behaviors to bring about a meaningful closure. "Closing a team prematurely," he said, "leaves unfinished business, while avoiding closure issues allows members the opportunity to suggest additional work that may or may not be relevant to keep the team together." Grace asked about how they might best recognize team performance. Irma requested that they take some time to discuss satisfaction issues. Ron suggested a symbolic ceremony when they completed the writing for their publication. Alex added that whatever they decided to do, it ought to be fun. The team was ready to adjourn. Before they left, Alex passed out a chart he had made summarizing the relationship between group development stages, team outcomes, and intervention focus. This chart is presented as Table 8.1. The team members agreed upon their next meeting date and time and then adjourned.

TABLE 8.1 *Relationship Between Group Development Stage, Team Outcomes, and Intervention Focus*

Group Development Stage	Task Team Outcome	Relationship Team Outcome	Intervention Focus	Too much Intervening	Too little Intervening
1. Forming	Commitment	Acceptance	Balanced structure	Narrowness	Wandering
2. Storming	Clarification	Belonging	Healthy conflict	Chaos	Apathy
3. Norming	Involvement	Support	Participative helpfulness	Overhelpfulness	Unhelpfulness
4. Performing	Achievement	Pride	Moderate risk taking	Gambling	Safety
5. Adjourning	Recognition	Satisfaction	Meaningful closure	Additional work	Unfinished business

Note: Adapted from C.L. Kormanski (1996a). "Group Development and Total Quality Management Teams," in S.T. Gladding (Ed.), *Group Counseling and Group Process* (pp. 111–113), Greensboro, NC: ERIC/CASS.

9

Conclusion

The artist in ancient times inspired,
entertained, educated his fellow
citizens. Modern artists have an
additional responsibility—to
encourage others to be artists.

—Pete Seeger

*I*n early May, the team gathered to discuss the adjourning stage of their writing project. Grace thought that some type of conclusion would be helpful to summarize the ideas discussed in the manuscript. Ron suggested that this summary might also include some possibilities for future explorations. Irma commented that those who read the publication might want to form their own project teams, not just for writing purposes but for all kinds of group endeavors. Alex proposed a plan for the summer. He outlined a sequence of steps that included completing the final writings, obtaining reviews by colleagues for the entire project, securing a publisher, and ending with a celebration event. Ron volunteered to begin the final segment of their writing by describing how teams can go about building a process model for addressing their particular needs. Grace wanted to explore the necessity, for any team, of collecting data and information. Alex thought that he would examine how teams move from planning to implementation. Irma chose to reflect on the future possibilities for teams and the challenges for team leaders. Later that month, they met to discuss their findings. Their summaries follow.

▼ BUILDING A PROCESS MODEL

Early in this book, individuals were encouraged to experiment with practice theories, taking ideas that have been presented and adding to them to create a model or theory that suits one's needs. To begin building a process model, one might start with ideas from Bolman and Deal (1984), who suggested three frames corresponding to basic organizational domains for the foundation. A symbolic frame includes shared values, a mission statement, symbols or logos, and a vision. The structural frame consists of goals, standards, and methods of measuring progress. The political frame involves issues, resources, groups, leadership style, and motivational needs.

To provide for interaction within this framework, Senge's (1990) five disciplines—mental models, personal mastery, team learning, shared vision, and systems thinking—are helpful. Mental models include, for example, Bolman and Deal's (1984) framework and can be enlarged by adding one's cultural and personal experiences along with those ideas contained in writings that help clarify the workplace. Personal mastery encourages us to acquire knowledge, develop skills, and become achievement motivated as we continue to provide temporary solutions for permanent problems. Team learning supports group problem solving, common goals, and continuous quality improvement. Shared vision describes the future of the team or other unit as well as energizes and empowers its members to become essential contributors to the desired outcomes. Finally, systems thinking is the integrative force that is characterized by interdependent working relationships, equifinality, open systems, and balanced change.

Transformational leadership (Burns, 1978) is the next ingredient. This inspirational and visionary leadership is often lacking in many organizations, as those in charge are preoccupied with operational issues and demands of the present. An organization that desires a future must have both the transactional leadership to address the current needs of the organization and the transformational leadership to develop the people who will shape its desired future. Early in the development of teams, transformational leaders clarify values, share organizational visions, and communicate through myth and metaphor. They also manage conflict in flexible and creative ways. Kaleidoscopic thinking, which involves looking at old problems in new ways, is a key skill in their arsenal. In the latter stages of team development, transformational leaders encourage networking, entrepreneurship, mentoring, and futuring. They also promote playfulness and humor. By prizing individual differences and enhancing multicultural awareness, they promote team member development and thus help the organization to be competitive in its future. Finally, transformational team leaders create celebrations and bring closure that aids in creating the myths and metaphors that are then communicated to new teams (Kormanski & Mozenter, 1987).

Adequate training for team leaders, facilitators, and eventually team members is also essential. Conyne, Wilson, and Ward (1997) described five areas of training that are important for team leaders and facilitators of task groups: (1) thinking interdependently and systemically, which is necessary for connecting the team to all parts of the organization and forward in time to the future; (2) recognizing the important role of performance and associated measures of outcome productivity as critical indicators of success; (3) including problem solving interventions as an essential role for the entire team; (4) developing facility in weighing intervention choices as the basis for selecting the leadership styles best matched to the followers' readiness levels to accomplish specific tasks; and (5) articulating core values that can be used as a criterion for judging organizational actions.

The Association for Specialists in Group Work (ASGW, 1991) identified task/work groups as one of four specializations in its professional standards for the training of group workers and delineated a set of knowledge competencies, a set of skill competencies, course work recommendations, and specific hours of supervised practice for this specialization. Using these standards, Conyne et al. (1997) established the following five clusters for instruction: teaching the definition of group work; pregroup preparation; therapeutic and leader skills; research and evaluation; and the ethical practice of task groups.

Models and theories, like everything else in the world, change over time. Radical changes are called paradigm shifts. Barker (1992) defined a paradigm as a set of rules and regulations that establish boundaries and describe how to behave inside the boundaries in order to be successful. A paradigm shift occurs when the rules change, necessitating a change in behavior to be successful. Moving from a national to a global marketplace is a recent example. Another is the perception of problems as permanent and requiring temporary solutions instead of attempting to develop permanent solutions for temporary problems.

Barker (1992) identified anticipation, innovation, and excellence as the keys for organizations to be successful in the future. The same concepts guide teams within organizations. Anticipation provides realistic expectations, innovation adds the continuous quality improvements, and organizational excellence sets the standards for achieving the vision. Once this paradigm is understood, transactional leadership provides the tools for managing within the paradigm. Innovation, however, may result in changing the rules, causing an organization to anticipate different outcomes and to reset its standards of excellence. This process creates a new paradigm and a resulting paradigm shift as the new model becomes superior to the old one by better explaining how to behave to be successful. During this transition, transformation leadership is required.

The rapidity of change in today's organizations creates increasing opportunities for paradigm shifts to occur. All paradigm shifts are not successful, however. Some, like picture telephones, occur too early; others, like space travel, move slowly as the needed technology is developed. Since existing models and explanations make one feel safe and comfortable, resistance to change is usually high. Moderate risk takers willing to accept modest failures are needed, as are high achievement-motivated teams. This is particularly true when the paradigm shift involves process models.

Engaging in the healthy conflict associated with change is only the first level of intensity. The second level occurs when conflict is pushed to the edge of chaos. Roger Lewin (1993) called this optimal paradigm complexity theory. This unifying theory states that all complex systems evolve from a few simple rules. The discovery of those rules begins with understanding the overall pattern and then identifying the root causes that produce the rules. This information provides the leverage to influence the change process.

▼ SCANNING THE ENVIRONMENT

Barker (1992) noted that a significant competitive advantage can be obtained by groups and individuals who anticipate well in turbulent times. A critical function for most teams is to heighten awareness by building an ongoing information-gathering process for collecting the data necessary for current decision making and for the strategic planning of the organization. Early in the life of a team, an assessment of the team's internal strengths and weaknesses and external opportunities and threats (called a SWOT analysis) is recommended as a prelude to issue identification and goal setting. Based on Lewin's (1951) work, this process provides a current description of a team's resources and needs as well as its external challenges.

Identification of critical issues is the next step. When translated into goals, these are the building blocks of team and organizational visions. Bryson (1988) described these critical issues as moving along a continuum from operational to strategic. Operational issues present a challenge now, have a narrow impact, are less costly, require few major changes, have an apparent solution or two, are mildly sensitive, and will cause some inconvenience if not addressed. Strategic issues are those that will present a challenge in the future, have a broad impact, are expensive, require major changes, have no obvious solutions, are emotional dynamite, and can cause disasters if not addressed.

For most teams a good amount of time is needed for addressing both operational and strategic issues. Teams must also monitor the issues, as each is moving developmentally from the strategic side to the operational side. This movement turns visions into reality. A regressive incident may create a backward movement when implementation is not possible and new solutions are needed. Of course, teams that are together for long periods of time may need to periodically revisit and add to the vision.

Once issues are identified and assessed, a trend analysis is in order. This process examines individual issues over time. The current state of an issue is described in terms of its political, economic, social, and technological aspects (commonly called PESTs). Most issues can be classified as being characterized by one or more of those four aspects (Pfeiffer, Goodstein, & Nolan, 1989). Past antecedent events are sought next. These are the triggers that have accelerated the trend and given it momentum. Once a team knows where a trend came from and what it looks like now, the members can project it forward and suggest future implications if interventions are not made now. The more operational the trend, the more quickly an intervention is needed. The more strategic the trend, the more understanding and thoughtful planning are required. Barker (1992) noted that because of this clear direction, the identification and analysis of trends helps reduce turbulence and chaos.

The following 20 trends affecting organizations in our society (Bennis & Mische, 1996; Lock, 1996; Naisbitt & Aburdene, 1990) suggest a need for cooperative teamwork, but some may require a different type of team than what is currently available:

POLITICAL

▼ Deregulation will increase competitiveness and risk.

▼ Personal power is replacing position power.

- ▼ Organizational loyalty will decrease along with job security.
- ▼ Hierarchies are being replaced by networks.
- ▼ A changing legal environment is providing for more equal opportunity.

ECONOMIC

- ▼ Quality is becoming paramount, and service is close behind.
- ▼ The part-time and temporary workforce will grow.
- ▼ More new jobs will be created by small businesses.
- ▼ Income gaps will widen.
- ▼ Self-employment will continue to increase.

SOCIAL

- ▼ Diversity and feminization of the workplace are increasing.
- ▼ More work will be done at home.
- ▼ Quality-of-life needs are gaining in importance.
- ▼ The mismatch between available jobs and people's skills will continue.
- ▼ Unemployment will remain high, and changing jobs will be a fact of life.

TECHNOLOGICAL

- ▼ Information is becoming our most valuable commodity.
- ▼ Continuous training will be needed to keep up with change.
- ▼ Computer skills are replacing literacy as a job requirement.
- ▼ Technology will decrease mundane tasks but will increase the amount of work employees do.
- ▼ Managers will have more time for teaching and coaching.

As work groups and teams increase in our organizations, another trend will be the increasing need for process consultants to provide the expertise and training discussed in this book (Kormanski & Eschbach, 1997).

A process that parallels environmental scanning, or data collection, involves implementation considerations (Pfeiffer et al., 1989). The data obtained from scanning are largely used for planning purposes but may also be relevant to the eventual implementation of the solutions. From environmental scanning, most teams discover small but significant needs that can be addressed quickly without elaborate planning if only someone with authority would take action. One organization created a "just do it" team with the CEO as sponsor. Over a few months' time, numerous interventions were made ranging from the installing shelves in restrooms for packages and purses to putting up identification and direction signs throughout the grounds and facilities.

As our society continues to move into the age of information, environmental scanning will increase in importance. Just as process feedback has been found to help internal group functioning and produce more successful outcomes, expanded sources of information will do the same. A new need, however, will be how to organize, evaluate, and make useful this huge new resource, which now arrives in a more sophisticated technological package.

▼ ENGAGING IN ACTION PLANNING

Goal setting is the critical skill that links the conceptual plan with the action of implementation. Lewin (1951) described the process by which groups within organizations identify and solve problems as action research. The process begins with data collection and diagnosis and ends with evaluation about a specific issue. The middle of the model is an action planning phase whereby goals are set, implementation strategies are selected and sequenced, methods of measuring progress are defined, and performance occurs. That basic model is still intact today, although it has been continuously improved.

McClelland (1961) identified the need for achievement as a motivator for high readiness individuals and described people with high achievement motivation as those who set goals that are challenging but realistic. This type of goal setter is a moderate risk taker who will accept modest failures. He or she views such failures as learning experiences. These high achievers are consistently successful about 60% of the time, desire performance feedback, take personal responsibility for task accomplishment, and develop comprehensive plans for goal achievement. Effective teams, composed of such members, try out temporary solutions and use early failures as constructive feedback for building better solutions over time. In sports, the greatness of a team depends on how well the team members perform after a loss.

Weisbord (1987) suggested the use of an organizational diagnosis model that identifies gaps between the present state and the desired state of the future. In this model, goal setting is a continuous process that recycles itself after each evaluation as members reset goals to continue to narrow the gap. Effective teams create critical success indicators to measure progress toward goals. These are usually posted on some type of scoreboard to act as a performance reminder for the entire team. Blanchard and Johnson (1982) suggested 1-minute goal setting to enhance performance and improve work relationships. Applied to a team approach, members would agree on goals and performance measures. Each goal would be written on a single sheet of paper and checked periodically to assess progress. By providing a behavioral measurement and a direction (i.e., improve, increase, or decrease), goals become operational and ready for implementation.

Robinson and Robinson (1995) advocated the use of both strategic goals and tactical goals for performance improvement. Strategic goals are long-term and address both internal (team or department) and external (customer or client) needs. Tactical goals are short-term and support strategic initiatives. They are more specific, include a measurement to make them operational, and have a date for accomplishment as well as an accountable person or team who owns the goal.

Locke and Latham (1990) pointed out that goals that are quantitative, challenging, and specific result in better performance. Furthermore, they found that the higher the goal, the higher the performance when other variables were held constant and goals were realistic. Self-confidence had an additive effect when difficult goals were combined with ability. Self-selected goals were found to be motivational and to encourage the search for more creative and suitable strategies. Goals without feedback were not very effective. According to these researchers, performance feedback makes goals trackable over time and allows for continuous improvement.

Varney (1989) encouraged the setting of both team and individual goals. He noted, however, that these goals must be clearly defined so that everyone understands them. For teams, shared goal setting at both the team and individual level is essential to the team building process. Commitment to the goals, an interdependent working relationship, and accountability through the measurement of progress are additional essential components of becoming a team (Reilly & Jones, 1974). In the organizational setting, support from the organization creates a higher level of interdependence and mutual benefits, since team performance contributes to the strategic initiatives of the organization. Within the team, individual goal accomplishment can provide for personal achievements and professional development.

Albrecht (1992) stated that when attempts are made to measure goals that assess quality, the discretion given to the team to achieve the outcome being measured must vary based on how objective the measurement method is. He noted four types of objective, or outcome goals and described effective measurement methods for each. First, managing risks ensures that important behaviors can be performed. The most effective measurement method is observation. Second, managing resources challenges teams to deliver the highest quality at the lowest cost. The measurement of procedures and processes requires a quality audit to examine a series of practices and how well people are following them. Third, managing tangibles ensures that the customer or client receives a service or item that functions properly based on preset standards. Counting specific successes is an appropriate means of keeping score and delivering a numerical total. Fourth, managing perceptions examines the feeling reaction, state of mind, or subjective value of the client or customer. This is the most difficult objective to measure over time. Frequently, customers and clients are surveyed using qualitative research methods to assess the strategies that are meant to provide satisfaction outcomes. Focus groups, case studies, and individual interviews are other qualitative methods currently in use. Measuring progress is always a challenge. Matching the measurement method and the measurement statistic with the outcome goal is critical.

▼ LIVING THE VISION

No matter what a team commits itself to achieving, the process of visioning provides a description of the ideal future. Block (1987) viewed developing a vision as the first step in gaining team autonomy. In a team, a discussion of vision invites ownership and involvement. Vision provides a framework within which goals can be formed to make the future a reality. This vision will guide the implementation of strategies to shape the future (Bryson, 1988).

Many visions begin as dreams. Thus, they are more abstract than concrete; more changeable than stable; and more individually owned than group owned. In addition, they can be fleeting and can easily become lost. Some visions constructed by groups, teams, and organizations have a specific purpose in mind. Strategic planning is one such example. These visions are formed as part of a process model. They evolve over time and reflect the group dynamics of the team. As the team scans the environment and collects data, issues are identified as targets for further examination and possible improvement. A vision provides a picture of the team's outcomes following the implementation of related goals and strategies.

Visions can be short and succinct, and thus more motivational than directive. Examples would be "Quality is king" and "People are our most important resource." Most visions, however, are thematic, complex, and dynamic. They are composed of a variety of themes that combine the critical issues of the team or organization that created them. They are complex, with components that range from being operational (ready to implement and have a direct impact) to being strategic (unclear solutions that need continued discussion). Finally, each component is dynamically changing. Those components that are moving developmentally are becoming more operational and those that are moving regressively are becoming more strategic. A series of jet planes landing at a busy airport is an apt example. Each landing of a jet represents the implementation of a component of the vision. A number of other planes await their turn to land. Sometimes the landing is postponed because of organizational constraints (only one available runway) and a circling pattern is necessary (a regressive movement requiring a strategic intervention prior to becoming operational). At other times, a crisis (a snowstorm or dangerous wind shear) may cause the plane to be diverted to another airport (much more strategic thinking required prior to an operational implementation). All visions, whether short and succinct or highly complex, should be inspirational.

Visions are about possibilities (Kouzes & Posner, 1987). They express optimism, and those who developed them hope their components become probabilities as they become more operational. They invite others to help make a difference. Once shared, they energize people. DePree (1989) suggested that a clear vision generates momentum. Team momentum makes the impossible possible. When the vision is communicated in a manner that encourages individuals to act, teams win when they were expected to lose.

Visions are about living. The Book of Proverbs tell us that without vision, people perish. A vision is spiritual, emotional, and positive. It comes from both the heart and the head. It ties the present to the future. It challenges team members to believe: to believe in the team and in oneself. A vision identifies the contributions all must make, not the personal rewards one will receive. It can build a common ground, promote inclusion, and encourage diversity. A vision provides opportunities for involvement for all team members in achieving team goals and celebrating team accomplishments. Visions need leaders because they are often abstract and initially lack specifics. Leadership provides the clarity and the details that enhance understanding and gain commitments.

Covey (1996) described three new roles for leaders. In a pathfinder role, the leader thinks strategically and constructs the plan that ties the vision, values, and mission to the stakeholder and customer needs. This role infuses the culture with a renewed sense of purpose and an exciting future. In an aligning role, the leader ensures that every member of the team and organization will support and work to implement the plan. Understanding needs is critical. In an empowering role, the leader encourages the synergy that is fueled by the talent, ingenuity, intelligence, and creativity of people. As results are achieved, celebrations and feedback continue the empowerment process and build future leaders.

Handy (1996) suggested that the best individuals to fill these roles are those who believe in themselves, possess a passion for the work, and have a love of people. He also noted that they must walk alone from time to time. Thus, inspirational and visionary leaders are often lonely during challenging periods but persist at moving forward and building momentum. As the crisis is resolved, team members can begin to share the leadership role.

The ultimate challenge is to continue to develop leaders. Teamwork meets this challenge on a grand scale. The results are not just a few great leaders but an infinite number of leaders at a variety of levels who create a never-ending process of leadership development that will ensure our future as a democratic society.

▼ TEAMWORK

By the end of the summer, the team's writing project had been completed. A publisher had confirmed an offer to publish the manuscript. Colleagues had reviewed it, and the publisher had begun the final editorial changes. The team was eagerly awaiting the final product.

Alex commented on how well the team development process had worked for them. Not only was the outcome a huge success, but the quality of the product gave all of them a feeling of satisfaction and pride. "Trusting the process," he said, "really works."

Grace suggested that shared leadership was an important factor. She noted that all of them had used their individual strengths and abilities for the benefit of the group. The leadership had rotated naturally based on situational needs. "Leadership," she said, "is the responsibility of everyone."

Irma identified the interdependent working relationship as a major contributor to their team effort. "Awareness gave us focus, conflict resulted in commitment, and cooperation provided the synergy," she noted. "But, the actual productivity occurred when high independence and high dependence occurred simultaneously. Interdependent team efforts increase momentum."

Ron proposed that vision was the unifying concept that provided them with direction and inspiration. "Vision aligns the team and the organization toward shared goals and a desired future," he added. "A vision creates a future, but one must live the vision."

The team planned a final celebration. As the discussion wound down, they all agreed that the guidelines they had just specified were essential for successful teams: trust the process, share the leadership, work interdependently, and live the vision. As they planned for adjournment, they reached the consensus that they were successful because they believed in *teamwork!*

References

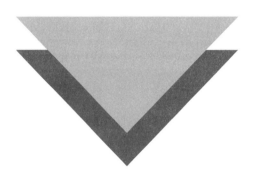

Albrecht, K. (1992). *The only thing that matters*. New York: HarperCollins.

Association for Specialists in Group Work. (1991). *Professional standards for the training of group workers*. Alexandria, VA: Author.

Baldridge, V. (1971). *Academic governance*. Berkeley, CA: McCutchan.

Bales, R. F. (1953). The equilibrium problem in small groups. In T. Parson, R. F. Bales, & E. A. Shils (Eds.), *Working papers in the theory of action* (pp. 111–161). Glencoe, IL: Free Press.

Bales, R. F. (1958). Task roles and social roles in problem-solving groups. In E. Maccoby, T. Newcombe, & E. Hartley (Eds.), *Readings in social psychology* (pp. 437–447). New York: Holt, Rinehart & Winston.

Barker, J. A. (1992). *Paradigms: The business of discovering the future*. New York: HarperCollins.

Barnard, C. I. (1938). *The functions of the executive*. Cambridge, MA: Harvard University Press.

Barr, L., & Barr, N. (1989). *The leadership equation: Leadership, management, and the Myers-Briggs*. Austin, TX: Eakin.

Bass, B. M. (1985). *Leadership and performance beyond expectations*. New York: Free Press.

Bennis, W. (1990). *Why leaders can't lead*. San Francisco: Jossey-Bass.

Bennis, W., & Mische, M. (1996). *The 21st century organization*. San Diego, CA: Pfeiffer & Co.

Bennis, W., & Nanus, B. (1985). *Leaders: The strategies for taking charge*. New York: Harper & Row.

Bennis, W. G., & Shepard, H. A. (1956). A theory of group development. *Human Relations, 9,* 415–437.

Bion, R. W. (1961). *Experiences in groups*. New York: Basic Books.

Blake, R. R., & Mouton, J. S. (1964). *The Managerial Grid: Key orientations for achieving production through people*. Houston, TX: Gulf Publishing.

Blanchard, K. H. (1984). *Situational leadership II*. Escondido, CA: Blanchard Training and Development.

Blanchard, K., & Johnson, S. (1982). *The one-minute manager*. New York: Berkley.

Blanchard, K., Zigarmi, P., & Zigarmi, D. (1985). *Leadership and the one-minute manager*. New York: William Morrow.

Block, P. (1987). *The empowered manager*. San Francisco: Jossey-Bass.

Block, P. (1993). *Stewardship: Choosing service over self-interest*. San Francisco: Berrett-Koehler.

Bolman, L. G., & Deal, T. E. (1984). *Modern approaches to understanding and managing organizations*. San Francisco: Jossey-Bass.

Brinson, J. A. (1996). Cultural sensitivity for counselors: Our challenge for the twenty-first century. *Journal of Humanistic Education and Development, 34,* 195–206.

Bryson, J. M. (1988). *Strategic planning for public and nonprofit organizations*. San Francisco: Jossey-Bass.

Burke, W. W., & Church, A. H. (1992). *Managing change: Survey participant report*. Pelham, NY: W. Warner Burke.

Burns, J. M. (1978). *Leadership*. New York: Harper & Row.

Carew, D. K., Parisi-Carew, E., & Blanchard, K. H. (1990). *Group development and situational leadership II: A model for managing groups*. Escondido, CA: Blanchard Training and Development.

Carter, R. T., & Parks, E. E. (1996). Womanist identity and mental health. *Journal of Counseling & Development, 74,* 484–489.

Cascio, W. F. (1986). *Managing human resources: Productivity, quality of work life, profits.* New York: McGraw-Hill.

Cass, V. C. (1984). Homosexual identity formation: Testing a theoretical model. *Journal of Sex Research, 20,* 143–167.

Chavez, L. (1994, February 21) Demystifying multiculturalism. *National Review,* pp. 26–32.

Chickering, A. (1969). *Education and identity.* San Francisco: Jossey-Bass.

Clark, D. (1987). *The new Loving Someone Gay.* Berkeley, CA: Celestial Arts.

Cohen, A. J., & Smith, R. D. (1976). *The crucial incident in growth groups: Theory and techniques.* LaJolla, CA: University Associates.

Conyne, R. K., Wilson, F. R., & Ward, D. E. (1997). *Comprehensive group work: What it means and how to teach it.* Alexandria, VA: American Counseling Association.

Corey, G., & Corey, M. S. (1993). *I never knew I had a choice* (5th ed). Pacific Grove, CA: Brooks/Cole.

Covey, S. R. (1996). Three roles of the leader in the new paradigm. In F. Hesselbein, M. Goldsmith, & R. Beckhard, (Eds.), *The leader of the future: New visions, strategies, and practices for the next era.* (pp. 149–160), San Francisco: Jossey-Bass.

Cronback, L. (1951). Coefficient alpha and the internal structure. *Psychometrika, 16,* 297–334.

Cross, W. E., Jr. (1971). The Negro-to-black conversion experience. *Black World, 7,* 13–27.

Cummings, P. (1981). *The power handbook: A strategic guide to organizational and personal effectiveness.* Boston: CBI Publishing.

Dana, D. (1984). The costs of organizational conflict. *Organization Development Journal,* Fall, 1984, pp. 5–7.

Fay, P. P., & Doyle, A. G. (1982). Stages of group development: *1982 Annual for Facilitators, Trainers and Consultants.* San Diego, CA: University Associates.

Ferguson, M. (1980). *The aquarian conspiracy: Personal and social transformation in the 1980s.* Los Angeles, CA: Tarcher.

Fiedler, F. E. (1967). *A theory of leadership effectiveness.* New York: McGraw-Hill.

Foushee, H. C. (1984). Dyads and triads at 35,000 feet: Factors affecting group process and aircrew performance. *American Psychologist, 39,* 885–893.

French, J. R. P., & Raven, B. (1959). The bases of social power. In D. Cartwright (Ed.), *Studies in social power* (pp. 118–149). Ann Arbor: University of Michigan Press.

Fuqua, D. R., & Kurpius, D. J. (1993). Conceptual models in organizational consultation. *Journal of Counseling and Development, 71,* 607–618.

Gable, D., & Kormanski, C. (1983, October). The situational manager: Four approaches to dynamic leadership. *Registered Representative,* pp. 46–48, 55.

Glickman, A. S., Zimmer, S., Montero, R. C., Guerette, P. J., Campbell, W. J., Morgan, B., & Salas, E. (1987). *The evolution of teamwork skills: An empirical assessment with implications for training* (Tech. Report No. 87-016). Orlando, FL: Office of Naval Research, Human Factors Division.

Good, L., Hill, T., & Blanchard, K. (1992). *The leadership bridge: Situational leadership II and the Myers-Briggs Type Indicator.* Escondido, CA: Blanchard Training and Development.

Greenlaw, P. S., & Kohl, J. P. (1986). *Personnel management: Managing human resources.* New York: Harper & Row.

Gretzky, W. (1993, May). *Computerworld,* p. 125.

Griggs, L. B., & Louw, L. L. (October 1995). Diverse teams: Breakdown or breakthrough? *Training & Development Journal,* pp. 22–29.

Hall, J. (1971, November). Decisions, decisions, decisions. *Psychology Today,* pp. 54, 86.

Halverson, C. B., & Cue'llar, G. (1996). Diversity and team development. In J. W. Pfeiffer (Ed.), *The 1996 annual: Volume 1. Training* (pp. 235–244). San Diego, CA: Pfeiffer & Co.

Handy, C. (1996). The new language of organizing and its implications for leaders. In F. Hesselbein, M. Goldsmith, & R. Beckhard (Eds.), *The leader of the future: New visions, strategies, and practices for the next era* (pp. 3–10). San Francisco: Jossey-Bass.

Hanson, P. G., & Lubin, B. (1988). Team building as group development. In W. B. Reddy & K. Jamison (Eds.), *Team building: Blueprints for productivity and satisfaction* (pp. 76–87). Alexandria, VA/San Diego, CA: NTL Institute/University Associates.

Hare, A. P. (1976). *Handbook of small group research* (2nd ed.) New York: Free Press.

Hastings, C., Bixby, P., & Chaudhry-Lawton, R. (1987). *The superteam solution: Successful teamworking in organizations.* San Diego, CA: University Associates.

Hellreigel, D., Slocum, J. W., & Woodman, R. W. (1986). *Organizational behavior* (4th ed.). St. Paul, MN: West.

Helms, J. E. (Ed.). (1990). *Black and white racial identity theory, research, and practice.* Westport, CT: Greenwood.

Hersey, P. (1984). *The situational leader.* Escondido, CA: The Center for Leadership Studies.

Hersey, P., & Blanchard, K. H. (1982). *Management of organizational behavior: Utilizing human resources* (4th ed.). Englewood Cliffs, NJ: Prentice-Hall.

Hersey, P., & Blanchard, K. (1996, June). Revisiting the life cycle theory of leadership. *Training & Development Journal,* pp. 43–47.

Hersey, P., Blanchard, K. H., & Natemeyer, W. E. (1979). Situational leadership, perception, and the impact of power. *Group and Organizational Studies, 4,* 418–428.

Herzberg, F. (1966). *Work and the nature of man.* New York: World.

Hill, R. E. (1975). Interpersonal compatibility and work group performance. *Journal of Applied Behavioral Science, 11*(2), 210–219.

Holland, J. (1973). *Making vocational choices: A theory of careers.* Englewood Cliffs, NJ: Prentice-Hall.

Hollander, E. P., & Offerman, L. R. (1990). Relational features of organizational leadership and fellowship. In E. E. Clark & M. B. Clark (Eds.), *Measures of leadership* (pp. 83–97). West

Orange, NJ: Leadership Library of America.

Horne, A. M., Jolliff, D. L., & Roth, E. W. (1996). Men mentoring men in groups. In M. P. Andronico (Ed.), *Men in groups* (97–112). Washington, DC: American Psychological Association.

House, R. (1971). A path-goal theory of leadership. *Administrative Science Quarterly, 16,* 321–338.

Huszczo, G. E. (1990, February). Training for team building. *Training & Development Journal,* pp. 37–43.

Ivancevich, J. M. (1974). A study of a cognitive training program: Trainer styles and group development. *Academy Management Journal, 17,* 428–439.

Jung, C. G. (1971). *Psychological types.* Princeton, NJ: Princeton University Press.

Kanter, R. M. (1983). *The change masters.* New York: Simon & Schuster.

Kaplan, S. R., & Roman, M. (1963). Phases of development in an adult therapy group. *International Journal of Group Psychotherapy, 13,* 10–26

Keirsey, D., & Bates, M. (1984). *Please understand me* (5th ed.). Del Mar, CA: Prometheus Nemesis.

King, P. (December 1989). What makes teamwork work? *Psychology Today,* pp. 16–17.

Kiser, A. G., Humphries, T., & Bell, C. (1990). Breaking through rational leadership. *Training & Development Journal,* pp. 42–45.

Kohlberg, L. (1981). *The meaning and measurement of moral development.* Worcester, MA: Clark University Press.

Kolb, D., Rubin, I., & McIntyre, J. (1984). *Organizational psychology: An experiential approach to organizational behavior.* Englewood Cliffs, NJ: Prentice-Hall.

Kormanski, C. L. (1982). Leadership strategies for managing conflict. *Journal for Specialists in Group Work, 7*(2), 112–118.

Kormanski, C. L. (1985). A Situational Leadership™ approach to groups using the Tuckman model of group development. In L. D. Goodstein & J. W. Pfeiffer (Eds.), *The 1985 annual: Developing human resources* (pp. 217–225). San Diego, CA: Pfeiffer & Co.

Kormanski, C. L. (1988). Using group development theory in business and industry. *Journal for Specialists in Group Work, 3,* 1, 30–43.

Kormanski, C. L. (1990). Team building patterns of academic groups. *Journal for Specialists in Group Work, 15,* 206–214.

Kormanski, C. L. (1994). Ten discoveries about change: Ideas from business for counselors. *The Journal for the Professional Counselor, 9*(2), 9–15.

Kormanski, C. L. (1996a). Group development and total quality management teams. In S. T. Gladding (Ed.), *Group counseling and group process* (pp. 111–113). Greensboro, NC: ERIC/ CASS.

Kormanski, C. L. (1996b). Team interventions: Moving the team forward. In J. W. Pfeiffer (Ed.), *The 1996 Annual: Volume 2. Consulting* (pp. 85–88). San Francisco: Pfeiffer & Co.

Kormanski, C. L., & Bowers K. L. (In review). "Building task oriented teams." Manuscript submitted for publication.

Kormanski, C. L., & Eschbach, L. (1997). From group leader to process consultant. In H. Forrester-Miller & I. A.

Kottler (Eds.), *Issues and challenges for group practitioners* (pp. 133–164). Denver, CO: Love Publishing Company.

Kormanski, C. L., & Mozenter, A. (1987). A new model of team building: A technology for today and tomorrow. In J. W. Pfeiffer (Ed.), The *1987 annual: Developing human resources* (pp. 255–268). San Diego, CA: Pfeiffer & Co.

Kottler, J. A. (1993). *On becoming a therapist* (rev. ed.). San Francisco: Jossey-Bass.

Kouzes, J. M., & Posner, B. Z. (1987). *The leadership challenge: How to get extraordinary things done in organizations.* San Francisco: Jossey-Bass.

Kroeger, O., & Thruesen, J. (1988). *Type talk,* New York: Delacorte Press.

Lacoursiere, R. B. (1980). *The life cycle of groups: Group development stage theory.* New York: Human Sciences Press.

Lawrence, G. (1982). *People types and tiger stripes.* Gainesville, FL: Center for Applications of Psychological Type.

Lewin, K. (1951). *Field theory in social science,* New York: Harper & Row.

Lewin, R. (1993). *Complexity: Life at the edge of chaos.* London: Orion.

Lock, R. D. (1996). *Taking charge of your career direction* (3rd ed.). San Francisco: Brooks/Cole.

Locke, E., & Latham, G. (1990). *A theory of goal setting and task performance.* Englewood Cliffs, NJ: Prentice-Hall.

Loevinger, J. (1976). *Ego development.* San Francisco: Jossey-Boss.

Machiavelli, N. (1952). *The prince.* New York: New American Library.

Mann, R. D. (1967). *Interpersonal styles and group development.* New York: Wiley.

Maslow, A. H. (1954). *Motivation and personality.* New York: Harper & Row.

Maslow, A. H. (1971). *The farther reaches of human nature.* New York: Viking Press.

McAfee, R. B., & Champagne, P. J. (1987). *Organizational behavior: A manager's view.* St. Paul, MN: West.

McClelland, D. C. (1961). *The achieving society.* Princeton, NJ: Van Nostrand.

McGregor, D. (1960). *The human side of enterprise.* New York: McGraw-Hill.

Miles, M. B. (1981). *Learning to work in groups* (2nd ed.). New York: Teachers College Press.

Mills, T. M. (1964). *Group transformation.* Englewood Cliffs, NJ: Prentice-Hall.

Moosbruker, J. (1987). Using a stage theory model to understand and manage transitions in group dynamics. In W. B. Reddy & C. C. Henderson, Jr. (Eds.), *Training theory and practice* (pp. 83–92). Alexandria, VA/San Diego, CA: NTL Institute/University Associates.

Myers, I. B. (1980). *Gifts differing.* Palo Alto, CA: Consulting Psychologists Press.

Myers, I. B. (1993). *Introduction to type* (5th ed.). Palo Alto, CA: Consulting Psychologists Press.

Naisbitt, J., & Aburdene, P. (1990). *Megatrends 2000: Ten new directions for the 1990's.* New York: William Morrow.

Ohme, H. (1977). Ohme's law of institutional change. *Phi Delta Kappan, 59* 263–265.

O'Neil, J. M., & Roberts Carroll, M. (1988). A gender role workshop focused on sexism, gender role conflict, and the gender role journey.

Journal of Counseling & Development, 67, 193–197.

Peters, T. J. (1987). *Thriving on chaos: Handbook for a management revelation.* New York: Knopf.

Pfeiffer, J. W., Goodstein, L. D., & Nolan, T. M. (1989). *Shaping strategic planning.* Glenview, IL: Scott, Foresman.

Piaget, J. (1970). *Science of education and the psychology of the child.* New York: Orion.

Pokora, J., & Briner, W. (1988). Outstanding performance through superteams. In J. W. Pfeiffer (Ed.), *The 1988 annual: Developing human resources* (pp. 215–222). San Diego, CA: University Associates.

Raven, B. H., & Kruglanski, W. (1975). Conflict and power. In P. G. Swingle (Ed.), *The structure of conflict* (pp. 177–219). New York: Academic Press.

Reese, B. J., & Brandt, R. (1987). *Effective human relations in organizations* (3rd ed.). Boston: Houghton Mifflin.

Reilly, A. J., & Jones, J. E. (1974). Teambuilding. In J. W. Pfeiffer & J. E. Jones (Eds.), *The 1974 annual handbook for group facilitators* (pp. 227–237). San Diego, CA: Pfeiffer & Co.

Robinson, D. G., & Robinson, J. C. (1995). *Performance consulting: Moving beyond training.* San Francisco: Berrett-Koehler.

Rogers, C. R. (1961). *On becoming a person: A therapist's view of psychotherapy.* Boston: Houghton-Mifflin.

Ryan, B. F., Joiner, B. L., & Ryan, T. A. (1985). *Minitab handbook* (2nd ed.). Boston: Duxbury Press.

Schein, E. H. (1985). *Organizational culture and leadership.* San Francisco: Jossey-Bass.

Schnall, M. (1981). *Limits: A search for new values.* New York: Potter.

Schutz, W. D. (1958). *FIRO: Three-dimensional theory of interpersonal behavior.* New York: Rinehart.

Schutz, W. D. (1982). *The Schutz measures.* San Diego, CA: Pfeiffer & Co.

Selznick, P. (1957). *Leadership in administration: A sociological interpretation.* New York: Harper & Row.

Senge, P. M. (1990). *The fifth discipline.* New York: Doubleday.

Shonk, J. H. (1982). *Working in teams: A practical manual for improving work groups.* New York: AMACOM.

Slater, P. E. (1966). *Microcosm: Structural, psychological, and religious evolution in groups.* New York: Wiley.

Solomon, L. N. (1977). Team development: A training approach. In J. E. Jones & J. W. Pfeiffer (Eds.), *The 1977 annual handbook for group facilitators* (pp. 181–193). San Diego, CA: University Associates.

Sundstrom, E., DeMeuse, K. P., & Futrell D. (1990). Work teams: Applications and effectiveness. *American Psychologist, 45,* 120–133.

Thelen, H., & Dickerman, W. (1949). Stereotypes and the growth of groups. *Educational Leadership, 6,* 309–316.

Tuckman, B. W. (1965). Developmental sequence in small groups. *Psychological Bulletin, 63,* 384–399.

Tuckman, B. W., & Jensen, M. A. (1977). Stages of small group development revisited. *Group and Organizational Studies, 2,* 419–427.

Vaill, P. B. (1989). *Managing as a performing art.* San Francisco: Jossey-Bass.

Varney, G. H. (1989). *Building productive teams: An action guide and resource book.* San Francisco: Jossey-Bass.

Vroom, V., & Yetton, P. (1973). *Leadership and decision making:* Pittsburgh, PA: University of Pittsburgh Press.

Waldo, M. (1985). A curative factor framework for conceptualizing group counseling. *Journal of Counseling and Development, 64,* 52–64.

Walton, M. (1990). *Deming management at work.* New York: Putnam.

Ward, D. E. (1982). A model for the more effective use of theory in group work. *Journal for Specialists in Group Work, 7,* 224–230.

Weber, R. C. (1982). The group: A cycle from birth to death. In L. Porter & B. Mohr (Eds.), *Reading book for human relations training.* Alexandria, VA: NTL Institute.

Weisbord, M. R. (1987). *Productive workplaces.* San Francisco: Jossey-Bass.

Weisbord, M. R. (1992). *Discovering common ground.* San Francisco: Berrett-Koehler.

Winston, R. B., Boney, W. C., Miller, T. K., & Dagley, J. C. (1988). *Promoting student development through intentionally structured groups.* San Francisco: Jossey-Bass.

Woodcock, M. (1979). *Team development manual.* New York: Wiley.

Woodcock, M., & Francis, D. (1981). *Organization development through team building: Planning a cost effective strategy.* New York: Wiley.

Yalom, I. E. (1985). *The theory and practice of group psychotherapy* (3rd ed). New York: Basic Books.

Zimpfer, D. G. (1986). Planning for groups based on their developmental phases. *Journal for Specialists in Group Work, 11,* 180–187.

Zurcher, L. A., Jr. (1969). Stages of development in poverty program neighborhood action committees. *Journal of Applied Behavioral Science, 15,* 223–258.

Index

readiness, 98, 101, 104, 109, 110
responsibility, 109, 111
Taylor, Frederick, W., 31, 97
Team(s)
  circular, 135
  compatibility, 146
  characteristics of, 137–139
  criteria for, 6
  development , 90, 133, 136, 180
  goals, 6, 7–8, 11, 57, 58, 59, 148, 203, 217, 219
  hierarchical, 135
  leadership, 134
  learning, 8, 9
  multicultural, 163–164
  role of, 9
  versus groups, 6–7
Team building, 133, 135, 217
Team Development rating Scale, 140, 142, 144, 147, 149, 150, 152
Teamwork, 4, 8, 32, 46, 74, 127, 135, 176, 220, 221
Temperament, 176–177
Thelen, H., 107, 108
Thinking, 161
  operational, 7
  preference for, 89
  strategic, 7, 50, 51, 52, 53, 219

systems, 8, 9, 210
Thruesen, J. 178
Time management, 109
Transcending dichotomies, 7
Transactional leadership, 48, 49, 71, 73, 74, 83, 84, 86, 88, 89, 98, 112, 119, 135, 169, 210, 211
Transformational leadership, 48, 49, 71, 73, 74, 75, 83, 84, 86, 88, 89, 98, 113, 134, 169, 210
Trend analysis, 213–215
Trist, Eric, 97
Trust, 97, 117, 121, 171
Tuckman (Bruce) model, 18, 36, 84, 140, 144, 162, 165, 166–167, 168, 171

Universality, 123

Vaill, Peter, 10
Values, 52, 79, 99, 219
  conflicts, 45–46
  core, 211
  leader, 69, 89
Varney, G. H. 134, 135, 217
Vision, 211, 219, 221
  shared, 8, 90, 195, 210
  statement, example of, 192

Visioning, 52, 76, 89, 148, 218–220
Vroom, V., 88

Waldo, M., 213
Ward, D., E., 111, 121, 210
Weber, R. C., 123
Weisbord, M. R., 10, 58, 71, 79, 97, 116, 216
Wilson, F. R., 210
Winston, R. B., 124
Withdrawal, as a strategy, 61–62, 65
Woodcock, M., 136, 139, 140, 144
Woodman, R. W., 74
Workplace
  crises in, 104, 105
  diversity in, 98, 165, 214
  minority cultures in, 166

Yalom, I. E., 123
Yetton, P., 88
Young, 139

Zigarmi, D., 101
Zigarmi, P., 101
Zimpfer, D. G., 122
Zurcher, L. A., 146